Hull Then & Now 2

Another look at Hull's heritage

Published by Carnegie Heritage Centre Ltd
c/o The Carnegie Heritage Centre
342 Anlaby Road
Hull
HU3 6JA

Registered in England & Wales no.06966992
Registered charity no.1131585

Research, compilation and design paul-gibson.com

Frontispiece • Stonemasons at work in 1904 carving one of the capitals for the columns that form the classical frontage of Hull's City Hall. The City Hall was the centre-piece of the city improvement scheme that created Queen Victoria Square, King Edward Street and Jameson Street, and was the vision of Hull's first City Architect Joseph Henry Hirst, who was also the architect of the former Carnegie Library

ISBN 978-0-9555569-2-0

Printed and bound in Great Britain by Butler Tanner & Dennis, Frome

1 Andrew Carnegie

Preface

The city of Hull has a rich pictorial heritage of postcards, photographs and Smith drawings dating from the nineteenth and the twentieth centuries. The variety of subject depicted is vast – streets, with or without people; buildings, well maintained or in decay; together with citizens, employed, unemployed or simply idling the time away at 'oss wash'. Many books have been published, with varying degrees of success, in attempts to bring together in image and caption a portrait of all or part of the town. To give a balanced portrait the selection of images must illustrate not only the fine frontages of major streets, as can be seen in Corporation official guidebooks, but must travel into the courts and squares behind these fine frontages where the living condition of the residents were often unsanitary and squalid.
The information in a caption must address what is shown in the image, the information being widely researched and accurate.
These latter requirements require an extensive knowledge and understanding of possible sources of information, and an awareness of possible sources of misunderstanding in the information they give.
In the extensive literature of Hull's local history I suggest that there are no better practitioners of the art of captioning than Chris Ketchell and the author and compiler of this book, Paul Gibson.

In ***Hull Then and Now 2*** Paul Gibson places in the public domain over 300 images of old Hull, generously drawing on his own collection to provide over 200 of these, many of great rarity, appearing in book form for the first time. The book supplements the author's earlier book ***Hull Then and Now***, travelling into areas of Hull away from the centre.

A great strength of the book is that many photographs show Hull's citizens against the background of the streets and buildings in which they lived their lives. Surely no series of photographs could capture better the atmosphere of these Hull streets in the later nineteenth and into the twentieth centuries. The author provides each group of photographs with a current photograph locating the scene today and an informative caption.

A great bonus in the book is the attention given to Joseph H. Hirst, Hull's first City Architect, appointed in 1900, and architect of the Hull City Hall, the old Police Station in Alfred Gelder Street and, indeed, the former Carnegie Library in which the publishers of this book are based. Hopefully more might come of this study at a later date.

Paul Gibson, author, compiler and generous provider of source material, and his associates deserve the greatest praise for the production of ***Hull Then and Now 2***, as must the Carnegie Heritage Centre be complimented for its publication.

Hull Then and Now 2 is a worthy successor to ***Hull Then and Now*** (2008) and ***The Anlaby Road*** (2007). Those who are fortunate possessors of either, or both, of these titles will need no further encouragement to buy this book.

Geoff Bell • April 2010

2, 3, 4 & 5 An example of the work of Joseph Henry Hirst was the Police Station in Alfred Gelder Street, constructed in 1902-04. The hammered granite plinth formed an imposing base for the building, which displayed strength in every detail, and the rusticated window and door details added further to the impression of security. The building was demolished when Littlewoods extended their Whitefriargate store in 1979; the store had originally opened in 1955, and the company had owned the old station since that date. A small part of the original building remains in the form of a side entrance in Parliament Street.

Contents

Introduction

The photograph used as the frontispiece for this book shows stonemasons hard at work on the finer details of the City Hall in 1904. Their work was enabled by the gifted man whose inspirational designs led to the construction of some of Hull's finest buildings, during a period in which no expense was spared and civic pride was upheld at all costs. All of the buildings shown in the introduction were designed by one man.

Joseph Henry Hirst was born in 1863, in the village of South Milford, on the outskirts of Leeds in West Yorkshire. Distant members of his family had been involved with the railway for decades, working on the construction of the Leeds and Selby Railway and the Hull and Selby Railway. By 1871 the Hirst family had moved to Hull, probably as a result of his father William's occupation; the 1871 Census recorded William as a railway signalman, aged 37, resident in one of the railway company's small houses near the Selby Street level crossing on the Anlaby Road. With him were his wife Mary Ann aged 32, his brother Charles, a railway engine driver aged 26, and his son Joseph Henry Hirst, aged seven and listed simply as a scholar.

In October 1880, at the age of 17, Joseph H Hirst had his first architectural drawing published in 'The House Decorator & School of Design' magazine. His often award winning architectural designs, would feature on the front of several other publications before he reached 20.
In 1887, when he was 24, Joseph Hirst was listed in the trade directories as an engineer, living in his own rented home at no.77 Derringham Street.
His engineering background may have come from his time spent with the Humber Volunteer Division of Submarine Miners, with whom he served from 1886 until 1893. He was later articled to civil engineer William H Wellsted, and in 1888 became an Inspector of Buildings for Hull Corporation Borough Engineers Department, based at the Town Hall. In 1892 he was created Building Surveyor and head of his own department, with a salary of £160 per year.

6 Stables and cart sheds for Hull Corporation Sanitary Department, Scarborough Street (1902)

7 Art Nouveau / Arts & Crafts Cabmen's shelter Hanover Square (1901-02) alongside the Town Hall, and others at various locations around the city.

In 1890 – then aged 27, Joseph married 28 years old Hannah Whitehead, at St Charles Catholic Church in Jarratt Street. Joseph and Hannah lived at Joseph's house in Derringham Street until at least 1893, and from 1897 until 1900 at no.109 Argyle Street. At that time he was still a council inspector, but in 1900 Hirst was appointed the first City Architect of Kingston upon Hull. By 1901, no doubt as a result of Hirst's success they were living at the newly built no.2 Belvoir Street, which he designed himself. He was listed there in the 1901 Census as City Architect, aged 37 with his wife Hannah, their two sons Joseph and William, and daughter Irene. Around 1907 they moved to a larger, and better quality house in Hymers Avenue; York Cottage, no.8 Hymers Avenue, was again designed by Hirst, and was their home until c.1930 when they moved across the road to no.47 Hymers Avenue.
Hirst was also a keen local historian and genealogist, having several local books published including a works on the Blockhouses of Kingston upon Hull and the 'Correct Arms of Kingston upon Hull'.

8 City Hall Queen Victoria Square (1903-09), probably Hirst's finest hour.

9 Villa Place School, Hessle Road (1907), demolished in the 1970s.

11 Joseph Henry Hirst c.1900

10 Rustenburg Street (seen here), Steynburg Street and houses fronting Newbridge Road (1902-03) for families displaced by the city centre improvement schemes.

Hirst remained the City Architect until 1926, when aged 63 he resigned his post, although he continued to work in private practice into his 70s. He died in 1945 aged 82, but his legacy is huge. Some of his well-known works, in addition to those shown within the introduction, are: Artisans dwellings, Great Passage Street (1900), new Market Hall & Corn Exchange (1902), West Park Lodge and East Park Lodge (1902), Scarborough Street Disinfecting Station (1902), Empress Hotel (1903), Fish Market, Corporation Field, Park Street, Fountain Road School (1904), Beverley Road Baths (1905), Endsleigh Training College, Inglemire Lane (1905), Pickering Park & Almshouses (1909 including the ornate wrought iron gates), Saner Street School (1909), Sidmouth Street School (1911), Southcoates Lane School (1911), Museum of Fisheries & Shipping Hessle Road (1912), Northern Cemetery Chapel, Chanterlands Avenue (1912), Castle Hill Hospital (as City of Hull Tuberculosis Sanatorium 1913), Open air school, Dairycoates (1913), Nautical School, Boulevard (1914), Newland School Cottingham Road (1914) and council housing estates in Preston Road, North Hull and Gipsyville.

1 • The Avenues

13 A writer in the Hull Packet of 11th September 1874 noted: 'I perceive that those extraordinary go-ahead builders, the Messrs. Garbutt, who have already done an immense amount of work on the Anlaby-road in the shape of street and house extension, have turned their attention to the land westward of the Park. They have I understand, purchased the whole of the land from near the Cemetery Gates to the bridge at what is known as Newland Tofts; and they are proposing to make an extensive boulevard, such as we have on the other side of the town, with 'circuses' and fountains. Simply draining, planting and laying out the land alone will cost £80,000. What the land has cost already is best known to the purchasers'. Reports such as this marked the slow start of the 'Westbourne Park Estate', now more familiarly known to us as 'The Avenues'. This 1904 photograph shows the entrance to Marlborough Avenue from Prince's Avenue with no.3 Stanstead Terrace on the left. Stanstead Terrace consists of six houses, three either side of Marlborough Avenue, although of slightly different designs.

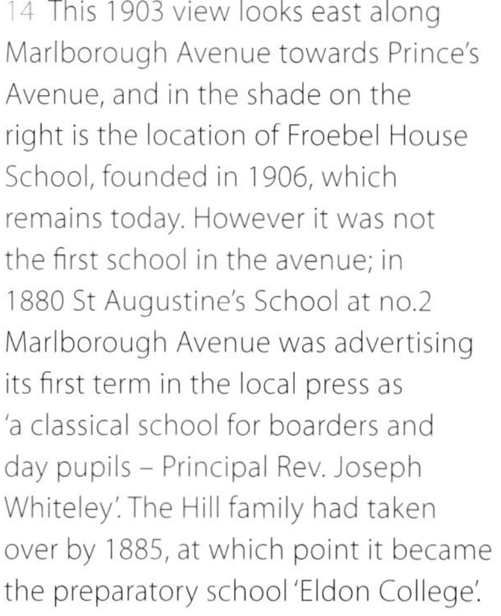

14 This 1903 view looks east along Marlborough Avenue towards Prince's Avenue, and in the shade on the right is the location of Froebel House School, founded in 1906, which remains today. However it was not the first school in the avenue; in 1880 St Augustine's School at no.2 Marlborough Avenue was advertising its first term in the local press as 'a classical school for boarders and day pupils – Principal Rev. Joseph Whiteley'. The Hill family had taken over by 1885, at which point it became the preparatory school 'Eldon College'.

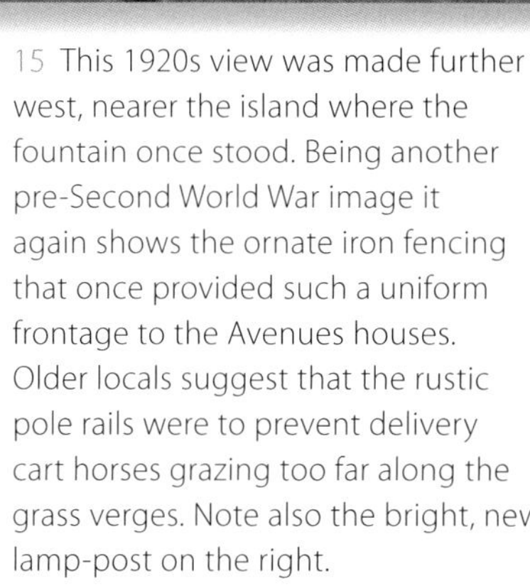

15 This 1920s view was made further west, nearer the island where the fountain once stood. Being another pre-Second World War image it again shows the ornate iron fencing that once provided such a uniform frontage to the Avenues houses. Older locals suggest that the rustic pole rails were to prevent delivery cart horses grazing too far along the grass verges. Note also the bright, new lamp-post on the right.

16 (Above) The Avenues developed slowly and sporadically, and an 1879 trade directory recorded just one occupied house in Marlborough Avenue, 13 in Westbourne Avenue, and none in either Park Avenue or Victoria Avenue. No.213 Marlborough Avenue was built as part of a terrace of 11 houses dating from c.1909. The ladies shown here in the front garden are Miss Irene White and her sister Margaret; the plate next to the door states 'Miss White' and the Kelly's directory of 1915 notes that Irene was a music teacher. The family remained in Marlborough Avenue for the another 50 years, Margaret remaining at no.211 until the late 1960s.

17 (Below) Marking the entrance to Westbourne Avenue, and refurbished during 2009, is this building – no.123 Prince's Avenue. This was formerly a more typical Avenues' property known as Westbourne House that was used as a nursing home in the 1930s, but was demolished following Blitz damage in the Second World War. This photograph dates from 1956, when on the 17th October that year Princess Alexandra of Kent made her first visit to Hull to open a new building on the site. The Young Women's Christian Association (YWCA House), was a hostel created to provide low-cost accommodation for young women who came to Hull seeking employment; it had 40 beds and cost £32,000 to build.

18 Westbourne Avenue was in many ways the showcase for the Westbourne Park Estate when it was first developed from 1874; by the time of the 1881 Census however, no more than 30 houses had been built, those on the south side, in the terrace between Richmond Street and the fountain (see page 15). By the time of Fryer's plan of Hull made in 1885, over three quarters of the land on the estate remained empty. An early obstacle that faced Mr Garbutt as he desperately tried to let his houses was the delay in getting gas lamps erected in the streets outside the newly built homes.

So desperate was Mr Garbutt by November 1877, that he offered to pay half of the cost of their supply. In his plea to the council at the time he said that he was 'about to considerably extend the buildings on the estate – in one avenue 40 houses were to be built, worth £3,000 each, and arrangements had been made for the laying out of several new streets. Most of the houses on the property for which he wanted the lamps were already let, and at present it was very dangerous for inhabitants at night'.

19 (Top of previous page) The Avenues' fountains did actually work from time to time, but from their earliest days there were problems. Stagnant water was often reported as a nuisance and the cost of running the fountains was criticised. In 1878 the cost of 'playing the fountains' for 15 days a year – for three hours each day, amounted to £20 including maintenance; but due to the complaints the fountains 'played' very infrequently. The remaining two fountains in Westbourne Avenue and Park Avenue were almost lost in 1926, when they were to be removed along with the Prince's Avenue fountains. Thankfully the motion was not passed by the council and the plan was rescinded.

20 (Main picture previous page) Another view of Westbourne Avenue, further east beyond the fountain near nos.64 and 66, and looking towards Prince's Avenue – the opposite view to picture 13. How peaceful it must have been in 1904 without the endless lines of parked cars and constant traffic.

21 (Below) The houses on the south side of Westbourne Avenue, between Richmond Street and the fountain, are shown here in 1904. The scene today, looking east towards Prince's Avenue, is almost unchanged except for the gas lamp – once for the benefit of pedestrians on the footpath, now a roadside feature to guide the motor car. These two elegant terraces contain some of the oldest houses in the Avenues', built c.1879, and remain virtually intact. In the distance are the towers of Tower House and Barcombe House – just visible behind. Barcombe House was built c.1879 for Edward Henry Garbett, general manager of the Hull Dock Company, and remained a private house until the 1930s when it became the Victoria Nursing Home. Tower House was initially unoccupied for many years, becoming a ladies' school in the late 1880s, which it remained until demolition c.1915. The site was then used for horticultural purposes by nurserymen G W Blackburn & Sons. The site of the matching houses is now more well-known as the Westbourne NHS Centre, utilising the surviving, although much-altered Barcombe House.

22 (Above) Salisbury Street in the winter of 1904. In the distance the Westbourne Avenue fountain and the matching towers of Barcombe House – in the centre, and Tower House to its right. The west side of Salisbury Street is the location of the Avenues' most distinguished houses, built to the designs of architect George Gilbert Scott junior in 1877-79. These were amongst the first houses to be built in the estate, and are contemporary with the twin 'tower' houses mentioned above.

23 (Left) The Avenues' famous fountains were made by King & Co of Hull in 1874 according to an article in the press at the time. The only surviving original fountain is that in Westbourne Avenue, which is now a Grade II Listed Building. This is the original Park Avenue fountain, looking north into Salisbury Street in 1904. Note that the east side of Salisbury Street was unbuilt at that time, with views through to the rear of property in Ella Street. Following an accident, the Park Avenue fountain was replaced with a modern imitation in 2001.

24 Many of the former grand houses in the Avenues' became too expensive to run for the average owner and from the 1950s many were converted for other uses, mostly as flats or care homes, but some as hotels. No.58 Park Avenue, seen here in 1915, is now a private hotel known as The Gables – but was constructed as a private dwelling c.1909.

25 (Above) The old chap taking a rest on the grass to the left of this 1904 photograph may have been a workman on the house that was being built there. This section of Park Avenue between Richmond Street and the fountain contains many similar houses mostly built c.1898-1900, some designed by Thomas Spurr.

26 (Above) The Park Avenue fountain c.1930, when the iron fencing around it had been removed and traffic levels were lower than today.

27 The matching terraces that wrap around Park Street, Salisbury Street west side, and into Victoria Avenue form one of the most attractive sections of the Avenues'. Initially named Park Villas, Salisbury Gardens and Victoria Villas, they were all built c.1887-89 and re-numbered as part of the main streets during the 1890s. This view of Park Villas is from 1903. To the rear of Park Villas in the 1880s, and covering most of the block between Park Avenue and Victoria Avenue, was a football ground, complementing the tennis courts of the Hull Lawn Tennis Club at the Prince's Avenue end of Westbourne Avenue, and the Polo ground at west end. The football ground – St Mary's club pitch, was mostly lost under the large gardens of the later Park Avenue and Victoria Avenue houses, and the east end was developed as Parkside Close in the 1960s.

28 (Above) The uniform appearance of this terrace in Park Avenue, was accentuated by the quality iron fencing that many modern residents would now dearly love. The seamless frontage is located between Richmond Street and Chanterlands Avenue, on the south side of the street (see also page 20).

(Below) This was the condition that one of the George Gilbert Scott Junior houses in Park Avenue had deteriorated to by the mid-1990s. It was rebuilt in 2000, and its neighbour refurbished, in a style that was sympathetic to the matching adjacent houses, and that retained the character of the area.

29, 30 & 31 A glimpse of life in Park Avenue around the time of the First World War, these photographs show scenes at 'Lynwood' – no.211 Park Avenue. Shown below, no.211 is part of a terrace of 20 houses, built on the south side between Richmond Street and the newly extended Chanterlands Avenue c.1910 (see page 19). The photographs were sent as postcards by the Sharp family in 1916, and local trade directories record that insurance agent Mr William Sharp was the resident of no.211 at that date. It is possible that he may have taken some role in the War effort, perhaps as a civilian worker, hence his arm-band. The scenes in the rear garden show that garden furniture is no new thing and the use of rustic woodwork was all the rage. Perhaps Mr Sharp also had one of the allotment gardens, established at the rear of these houses in the 1920s.

32 & 33 Salisbury Villas were the only houses built in the section of Salisbury Street shown in the 1904 photograph below. The land on the left – the east side of the street, remained open just a few more years before being built upon as we see it today.
The picture on the left shows the opposite view looking towards Ella Street c.1920. The houses on the left in the 1920 view were built on the front garden of Newland Tofts House, which faced east across Salisbury Street – one of many houses and farms in the area to take their name from the land on which they were built.

The Victoria Avenue fountain, like the Marlborough Avenue fountain, was of a more modest design to those in Westbourne and Park Avenue. It was removed c.1926 with those in Prince's Avenue.

34 (Right) The more modest housing at the west end of Victoria Avenue, was built during the 1920s, and includes Victoria Avenue's only side terraces – Regina Crescent, Victoria Gardens and Whitehall Gardens. This c.1930 view looks east along Victoria Avenue towards the Richmond Street junction.

35 (Below) On the left of this 1904 view is the end of the oldest terrace of houses in Victoria Avenue; nos.1 to 13 dating from c.1887. Picture 36 on the next page shows the opposite view.

36 In 1899 there were just 19 houses in Victoria Avenue, 18 on the south side and just one occupied property on the north side named Carlston House. Now no.48 Victoria Avenue, this was built c.1898 as one of a pair of matching red-brick houses with projecting first floors. The first occupant of no.48 was Mathew Thomlinson, general manager of the Hull Forge Iron & Steel Co. Just ten years later there were 55 houses on the north side and 62 on the south.

This photograph shows the avenue at the peak of this growth, in the opposite view to picture 35. Taken slightly further west along Victoria Avenue, and facing east towards Prince's Avenue, it was almost certainly taken the same day in 1904, as it shows several of the same children at play. On the left are gaps in the building line that were soon be filled with houses, including the imposing terrace of three-storey houses (nos.12 to 18) with jettied upper floors; built in 1905, these were designed by John Dossor.

37 Though not part of the Avenues' initial development it is hard to discuss the Avenues' without mentioning Chanterlands Avenue, which now provides more of a shopping area for local residents than Prince's Avenue. Taking its name from a 12th Century field name 'Chantergang' literally the Chanter-Lands, the road was begun from the Spring Bank West end in the late 1890s. Initially it stretched just as far as Perth Street and its development north was held back slightly by the Holderness Polo Club whose ground was located at the bottom of Marlborough Avenue and Westbourne Avenue (see facing page).
However, at a meeting of the Works Committee in November 1908 a plan was agreed for: 'a continuation of Chanterlands Avenue across the Polo Ground by a street of 40 feet wide only and for continuations of Marlborough Avenue, Westbourne and Park Avenue'. Why the extension was 10 feet narrower than the initial stretch is not known, but the kink in the road width can still be noticed near the Perth Street junction.
By February 1910 the extension of the avenues was complete, and Chanterlands Avenue extended to its next physical boundary – the Hull & Barnsley Railway's high-level railway line at the end of Victoria Avenue.

The north end of Chanterlands Avenue was laid out from Cottingham Road on the line of an old path known as Far Salt Ings Lane. The two sections were joined in 1923 when an underpass was created beneath the railway lines. The underpass can be seen in this late 1920s photograph looking north, with the entrance to Victoria Avenue on the near right.

38 & 39 Polo began in Hull with the Holderness Polo Club, who's initial ground was at Tranby Croft in Anlaby. A new ground west of the developing suburb of the 'Avenues' was laid out c.1896, in an area that already had tennis courts and football pitches, the first match played on Saturday 9th May 1896. These c.1900 photographs show the Polo ground at the peak of its popularity, when it regularly had attendances of over 5,000 people. The open nature of the area allowed many a free view, but most paid either sixpence or a penny. Sheets prevented the free views at later games, but scuffles between those in the cheaper area and those in the more expensive areas were a regular occurrence, as no real barriers prevented audience members from straying from one to the other.
The further development of the area signalled the end of the Polo Club, and the last matches were played in 1907. Chanterlands Avenue was extended north from November 1908 and new streets were built on the Polo ground. A reminder of the ground can be found in a terrace off Perth Street West – named Polo Villas.

40 (Above) Old and new images depicting a recurring problem. For those of us who suffered in the floods of 2007 there can be some reassurance in the fact that this was nothing new. These two photographs show Chanterlands Avenue and the underpass in the 1940s, and in the floods of June 2007.

41 A tram glides north along Chanterlands Avenue just beyond Goddard Avenue in the late 1920s. Trams were replaced by trolley buses in Hull from 1937 and some surviving trolley bus columns can still be seen in this area.

42 (Above left) The newly extended Chanterlands Avenue had many purpose-built shops such as this branch of William Jackson & Son, which opened in 1928 and is shown here soon after opening. From 2004 this became known as Sainsburys at Jacksons.

43 (Left) In April 1933 architect Frederick Robson drew plans on behalf of Moors' & Robson's Breweries for '1 house & hotel to be named the Avenue Hotel'. Local builder R G Tarran completed the building works on 27th December 1933 at a cost of £4,189-2s. Fred Fraser was the first manager of the pub, its licence transferring from the Dog & Duck in Wincolmlee, which closed in February 1933. The Avenue remains Chanterlands Avenue's only pub and is shown here in the 1940s before the many alterations and additions that have taken place in more recent years.

44 Many traditional independent shops survive on Chanterlands Avenue, such as butchers, cycle shops, cobblers and fruiterers despite our tendency to shop at the huge convenience superstores. Many of these had begun life as private houses such as no.16 Chanterlands Avenue, at the corner of Wharncliffe Street. Built around 1903 it was a private house until c.1908 when the house front was converted to a shop and fruiterer John Bainton began trading. The photograph here dates from c.1920 when Harold Storr Taylor had taken over the shop, by then the 'Radiator Fruit Stores', acknowledging the National Radiator Cos. factory in nearby National Avenue, established in 1905. The shop remained a fruiterer's until the 1950s, by which time competition was stiff with no less that seven fruit shops in the avenue, and it became a wardrobe dealer's shop. More recently its has been converted back to private accommodation.

2 • Prince's Avenue

46 & 47 As you turn out of Spring Bank, right into Prince's Avenue, it has become customary to glance in the window of the Gwenap shop to see what humorous items are on display. However, a more sombre view would have greeted the passer-by until the Edwardian era, as shown here. The Hull General Cemetery Co was formed in 1845 and its landscaped cemetery in Spring Bank was opened in 1847. The entrance lodge was constructed to the designs of architect Cuthbert Brodrick soon after, with extra buildings and alterations c.1853. Cemetery superintendent Michael Kelly is shown at the rear of the lodge (his private residence) with his wife Emmy – both are buried in the cemetery. He can also be seen at the cemetery gates in the larger photograph, both dating from c.1905. Note the railway signals that are visible in the smaller photograph, relating to the Botanic Gardens Station on the opposite side of Prince's Avenue.

48 (Below) The most northerly of the cemetery buildings is shown here c.1910, alongside the existing row of dutch-gabled shops that were built in 1907. The curving corner buildings (see above) were built in 1926-27 as this corner was widened to accommodate increasing traffic levels. Only the cemetery gates were saved, and removed to their present location in Spring Bank West. Shop no.3 was occupied by 'Gwenap ladies outfitters' from 1928.

49 & 50 (Above) Botanic Gardens station was built in 1864 to serve the York & North Midland Railway Cos. Victoria Dock branch line, laid out in 1852. The level crossing and signal box are shown above (left) in the 1950s and the station itself (right) just before closure in 1968. The Old Zoological pub, which opened in 1994, now occupies this site. This ever-changing road junction was once again redeveloped in Spring 2010.

Nat. Tel. 300x.

TAYLOR BROTHERS,

High-Class Grocers, and Provision Merchants,

Tea and Coffee Specialists,

Prince's Avenue, HULL

(Opposite Botanic Gardens Station).

COUNTRY ORDERS CARRIAGE PAID.

T. W. SCARR,

Hosier, Hatter, Glover and Shirt Maker,

GENERAL & SPORTS OUTFITTER,

17 PRINCES AVENUE, HULL.

Nat. Tel. 295x. (Opposite Botanic Station).

Outfitter to the Hull and Barnsley Athletic Club.

We hold the largest and Most Up-to-date Stock of **MEN'S WEAR in the district.**

Try our Collars, all Shapes, One Price, 6d. each, 2/9 ½-doz.

51 & 52 The Botanic area thrived due to the many new streets that were being built along Prince's Avenue, and very often where there was a station shops were built very soon after.
The terrace of 19 shops, nos.7 to 43 Prince's Avenue, included a wide variety of trades, some of which are shown here c.1915. Taylor Brothers 'high class grocers & provision' shop remained a grocers until the 1940s, later merging with no.13. No.17 was initially a confectioner's until hosier Tom Scarr took over c.1915. No.17 was later home to amongst others, a picture frame maker in the 1920s and a costumier in the 1930s.

A century later and no.13 latterly merged with no.15 as a 'tanning centre' (now closed); not a service most Edwardians would have required. Pollyanna - a gift shop established in May 2006, is now at no.17, having moved from no.27 (see page 33). However, Israel Utal, the 1930s costumier at no.17 is remembered in the sign that remains painted on the dutch gable end.

Nat. Tel. 4100x.

FRANK TAYLOR,

THE PRINCES AVENUE FRUITERER,

(Opposite Botanic Garden Station),

HULL.

Choose your Fruit from the Window. Everything of the :: :: best at Market Prices. :: ::

WREATHS AND CROSSES MADE TO ORDER,

by the most experienced hands in the City.

Satisfaction and prompt delivery Guaranteed.

TAKE CARE OF YOUR HAIR.

Consult the

"Maison Andrews,"

— *HULL'S LEADING HAIR SPECIALISTS.* —

29 PRINCES AVENUE, (*Opposite Botanic Station*)

NUMEROUS LOCAL SUCCESSES.

Manicure, Face Massage, Marcel Waving.

Nat. Tel. 598.

53 & 54 Frank Taylor took over a former bootmaker's when he opened his fruit shop at no.27 around 1914. The premises remained a fruit shop until the 1970s at least, when in 1972 there were three others in the street. Although we could do without a tan, we did however take care of our appearance. No.29, a hairdresser's from opening, was offering 'manicures, face massage and marcel waving' in 1915, and remained a hairdresser's until the 1970s at least. Several of the shops in this terrace retain original details but have suffered over the years from being built over old ditches and with little if any foundations.

In April 2010 no.27 was vacant as Pollyanna had moved to no.17 in 2009. No.29 was an Oxfam charity shop from c.1995 until very recently, and is now a beauty salon - reverting to its original use over 100 years later. Other shops in the terrace are of long-standing, such as no.7 which has been used by florists since the late 1930s. Florist' L E Hebblewhite have been here since the 1950s.

55 (Left) Prince's Avenue was developed in tandem with the Avenues estate, and was officially opened and adopted as a public highway on 3rd March 1875. Newland Tofts Lane, an old agricultural lane that ran alongside the Derringham Dike had been here for centuries, its alignment marking the boundary between Hull on the east, and the parish of Cottingham on the west. It was impassable for much of the year and a speaker at the opening ceremony of the Avenues noted 'Mr Garbutt had turned what had been a wilderness into a garden; a perfect Slough of Despond into a noble boulevard, a stinking stagnant ditch had given place to fountains of pure water and suburban villas'. By 1879 just 13 of them were occupied. This c.1910 photograph shows the corner of Welbeck Street to the left with grocer Thomas Peacock's shop on the corner. This block of six shops was built in 1899, and Welbeck Street was itself also laid out from 1899, when there were just 12 houses built.

56 On the opposite corner of Welbeck Street are three shops set at a different angle to the other dutch gabled shops. Now nos. 45 to 49 Prince's Avenue, they were built in 1899 as private houses, converted within a few years by the addition of single–storey shops over the small front gardens. No.47 is shown here in 1930 when it was newly opened as a wallpaper dealer's shop. In 2010 it is the Tropicana restaurant, incorporating no.45 next door. No.49 has now been a baker's shop continually for over a century, the first occupants of the shop being bakers Jane & Katherine Adam around 1907.

57 The streets that make up 'The Dukeries' – Welbeck, Thoresby, Clumber, Belvoir, Blenheim, Chatsworth and Hardwick, were named in 1897 during an era when thematic names were very popular, but the streets were not fully built upon until the early 1900s. Seen here around 1904 is Clumber Street looking west, and it is typical of the streets on this side of Prince's Avenue with its long regular terraces of simple working class homes. All of the property on the west side of Prince's Avenue is laid out on former farmland belonging to several farms that are shown on the 1850s and 1880s Ordnance Survey plans. One of these was part of the 230 acres of land purchased by David P Garbutt in 1874 upon which he developed the Avenues estate, described as: 'four closes of land situate in Newland Toft in the parish of Cottingham ... adjoining on a road lately known as Newland Tofts Lane or Princess Bank and then called Prince's Avenue ... also that messuage, tenements, or dwelling house used as a farm with the stables cowhouse barn shed and outhouse.'

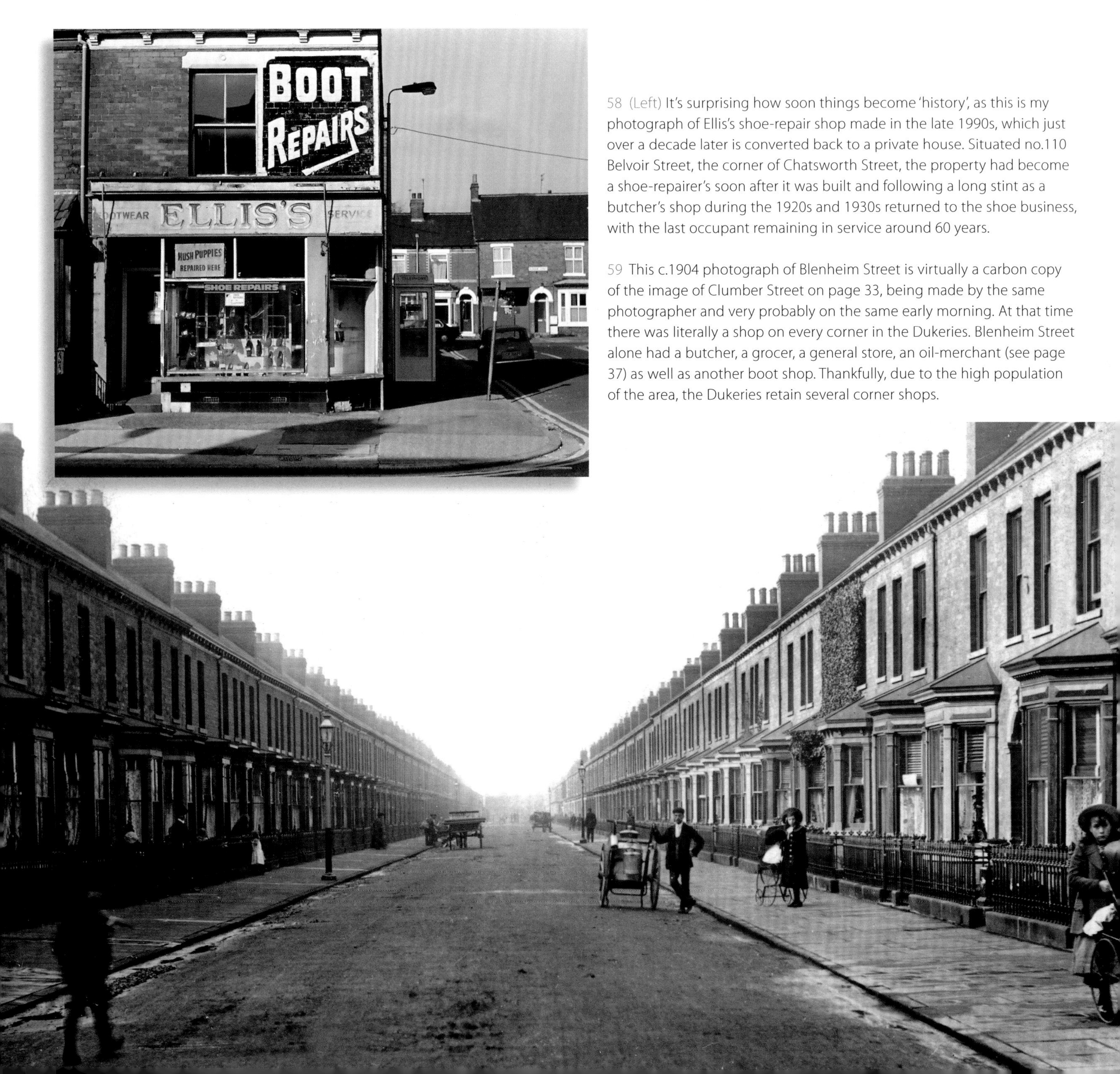

58 (Left) It's surprising how soon things become 'history', as this is my photograph of Ellis's shoe-repair shop made in the late 1990s, which just over a decade later is converted back to a private house. Situated no.110 Belvoir Street, the corner of Chatsworth Street, the property had become a shoe-repairer's soon after it was built and following a long stint as a butcher's shop during the 1920s and 1930s returned to the shoe business, with the last occupant remaining in service around 60 years.

59 This c.1904 photograph of Blenheim Street is virtually a carbon copy of the image of Clumber Street on page 33, being made by the same photographer and very probably on the same early morning. At that time there was literally a shop on every corner in the Dukeries. Blenheim Street alone had a butcher, a grocer, a general store, an oil-merchant (see page 37) as well as another boot shop. Thankfully, due to the high population of the area, the Dukeries retain several corner shops.

60 (Left) Another of Belvoir Street's original corner shops is shown here c.1910 – one of Mallorys oil merchants' 12 shops in Hull. This was no.203, on the corner of Hardwick Street, which is now a convenience store.

61 (Below) The Co-op won awards for its window displays and its not hard to see why. This is branch no.12 situated at the corner of Clumber Street and Prince's Avenue. Built in 1898, it was Work Brothers 'cash-grocers' until 1903 when the Co-op took over, remaining here until 1970. Latterly it has been the venue for different types of cuisine, the latest being the Giant Panda Chinese restaurant.

62 Opposite the Dukeries, on the east side of Prince's Avenue is a terrace (now nos.12a to 28) named Bickleigh Villas illustrated by the surviving name plate at the south end. All but one (12a) built 1891-92 as private houses with front gardens, from 1908 the houses gradually lost their shrubs and fences as the downstairs rooms were converted to shops. The huge increase in population brought about by the construction of the Dukeries, and the streets running through to Chanterlands Avenue, created a demand for more and more shops, which could only be situated in the larger main road properties. Seen here in 1909 is Hohenrein's pork butchers at no.20, who also had a shop in Waterworks Street. Latterly the Hull Food store in the 1990s, this is now part of the PAVE cafe-bar, which occupies nos.16 to 20 Prince's Avenue. The outdoor seating area in front of PAVE and the other bars along this stretch are all made possible as they fall within the extent of the original gardens of each house.

63 & 64 Just a few doors north of Hohenrein's was the newly opened shop of hairdresser John Mackenzie at no.26 Prince's Avenue; MacKenzie & Holborn were hairdressers in Tyler's Buildings, King Edward Street in 1905, but this branch was nearer his home address in Lambert Street. Incredibly, and similar to several others in the Avenue, this shop remained a hairdressers for almost a century, finally closing as the Prince's Salon – still a gents hairdresser, in the late 1990s. The interior and exterior of the shop are shown here c.1910 just before opening, but have now inevitably been converted to form part of Lounge, another of Prince's Avenue's cafe-bars, at nos.26 to 28.

65 All of the property leading to the corner of Duesbery Street, including the terrace known as Bickleigh Villas (the location of Lounge, PAVE etc), the Linnet & Lark pub and the former Fish Street Memorial Congregational Chapel, are built on the site of Alfred Martin's 'Park Nurseries'. The two houses set back from the road alongside the present petrol station were built in 1860 for Martin, Shaw & Sons – 'nurserymen, florists and seedsmen' of Junction Street in the city centre. Martin lived in one of them, known as Providence House, and these are now the oldest surviving houses in Prince's Avenue.

The nursery land was redeveloped from c.1890 and at the end of Bickleigh Villas two semi-detached houses were built, shown on the right of this 1904 photograph. In the early 1920s the Field Brothers – Sidney and Herbert – converted the houses and the former builder's yard at the rear, to a Taxi business and the Avenue's first all night petrol garage.

The motor trade remained here, and the site was latterly a car showroom until c.1990; the very popular Linnet & Lark pub was built here in 1994 as Prince's Avenue's first and only pub – how things have changed.

66 (Right) Duesbery Street was laid out in the early 1880s with just two detached houses on the south side; Duesbery House, which survives with its old coach house now converted to accommodation, and Coblentz House now demolished. The present terraced housing was built in 1898.
Shown here in 1904, the Fish Street Memorial Congregational Chapel officially opened in 1900 with seating for 700. Designed by W H Bingley, the church cost £7,000 including the £900 paid for the land, and had taken two years to build. The Elim Pentecostal City Temple took over from c.1984, and it is now known as the Church on the Way.

The Police Call Box in the centre of the picture was erected here in February 1930, and was removed in the 1950s. The all-night garage can also be seen, just to the right of the Police Box.

67 September 1931, looking back towards the church at the corner of Duesberry Street. On the left the terrace of houses built 1897-98 had been converted to small businesses and shops by the start of the First World War. A branch of the London & Joint Stock Bank opened at no.60 around 1907, latterly a Midland Bank, which closed c.1991. The second bank in the block was the Yorkshire Penny Bank, shown here on the corner, which opened in the early 1920s and remains today.

68 (Below) Park Grove was laid out in the early 1880s forming a link to Beverley Road via the earlier Park Road and Cave Street, and is shown here in 1904. At the south side of the entrance to Park Grove were four purpose-built shops, of which only three survive, one having been demolished following Blitz damage in the Second World War.

69 (Above) No.60 Prince's Avenue, is one of the three remaining shops built facing the fountain at the end of Park Grove c.1898. Initially a grocer's shop, by the 1930s this was the shared shop of fishmonger John Hudson and butcher George Taylor, both shown in this c.1939 photograph. More recently it has become a shop selling clothing and other goods, known as 'Ababil'.

70, 71 & 72 The only building in Park Grove other than private housing, was the 'French Convent', more correctly the Roman Catholic Convent of the Canonesses Regular of St Augustine Girls' School. This was an independent day and boarding school where girls from Roman Catholic and non-catholic backgrounds were educated to 'A' level standard. The Canonesses had fled to Hull from Versailles following the French anti-clerical laws of 1904 and founded the Park Grove school in 1906-07. The convent school also acquired three houses in Pearson Park, adjoining the college land.

The houses were Southside, Linden House – used as the convent villa for 'ladies who wished to live in the convent grounds' and Willersley House – the 'convent cloister'. The convent closed in 1972 having been found to be structurally unsafe, and was demolished in 1975, including its four houses within Pearson Park.
The site was later redeveloped for housing known as Convent Court, where most of the original wall and iron railings can still be seen along the main road side, alongside more modern railings made in a style that compliments the originals. All of the photographs shown here date from c.1910.

73, 74, 75 & 76 The boarders or pupils of the convent school wore a distinctive uniform bearing the badge of the school, which showed a cross overlaid with a lily in gold on a blue background. The drawings below are taken from a 1920s booklet produced by Hammonds in Hull who supplied the many items of 'obligatory' uniform as well as many sundry items over and above the uniform suggested 'for boarders only'. An 'old gold' beret was worn in winter and straw boater in the summer months. The Navy Union Raincoat seen below was a snip at 25 shillings and six-pence, the Navy felt hats eight shillings and eleven-pence, and the Blazer 27 shillings and six-pence. Dancing pumps in 'black glace Kid' were five shillings and eleven-pence, tan Willow calf walking shoes were 16 shillings and three-pence and goloshes were three shillings and eleven-pence a pair.

FROCKS FOR BOARDERS

Robes des élèves du Pensionnat.

NAVY BLUE FROCK for Best Wear in Fine Serge, Rep or Charmelaine.

The Collar and Tie for Trimming are of ciel blue Crepe de Chine, and are detachable. No other trimming is allowable except a little narrow black silk braid.

(Sketch on right.)
WHITE FROCK for occasional wear preferably in Washing Silk (Japschan) Crepe de Chine.

This style has been selected as suitable for the occasions on which the Frock will be worn, as well as being easily laundered or cleaned.

DANCING FROCK

Pupils who join the Winter DANCING CLASSES are advised to wear a Frock similar to this sketch, which may be in white, lemon, pale blue or pale pink Silk Taffetas with :: :: Knickers to match. :: ::

Every Pupil is expected to wear a Navy Blue Coat in simple tailored style as the above sketch (right).

- - - - - -

This can be made to measure by Hammond's or purchased ready-made. (Costume Department)

GYMNASIUM OUTFIT

French Convent.

(See Price List for Cost of Materials).

Pleated TUNIC in Navy Serge.
KNICKERS to match.
Braid GIRDLE to match.
White Shirt BLOUSE.
Brown STOCKINGS.
White Canvas SHOES, Rubber Soles.

Price (for making only) by HAMMOND'S, LTD.
Tunic, Knickers and Blouse 22/6

BLAZER in Navy Flannel, with School Badge, very useful for the Summer Term.

SCHOOL HATS in Navy Felt or Fur Felt can be fitted in Hammond's Millinery Department.

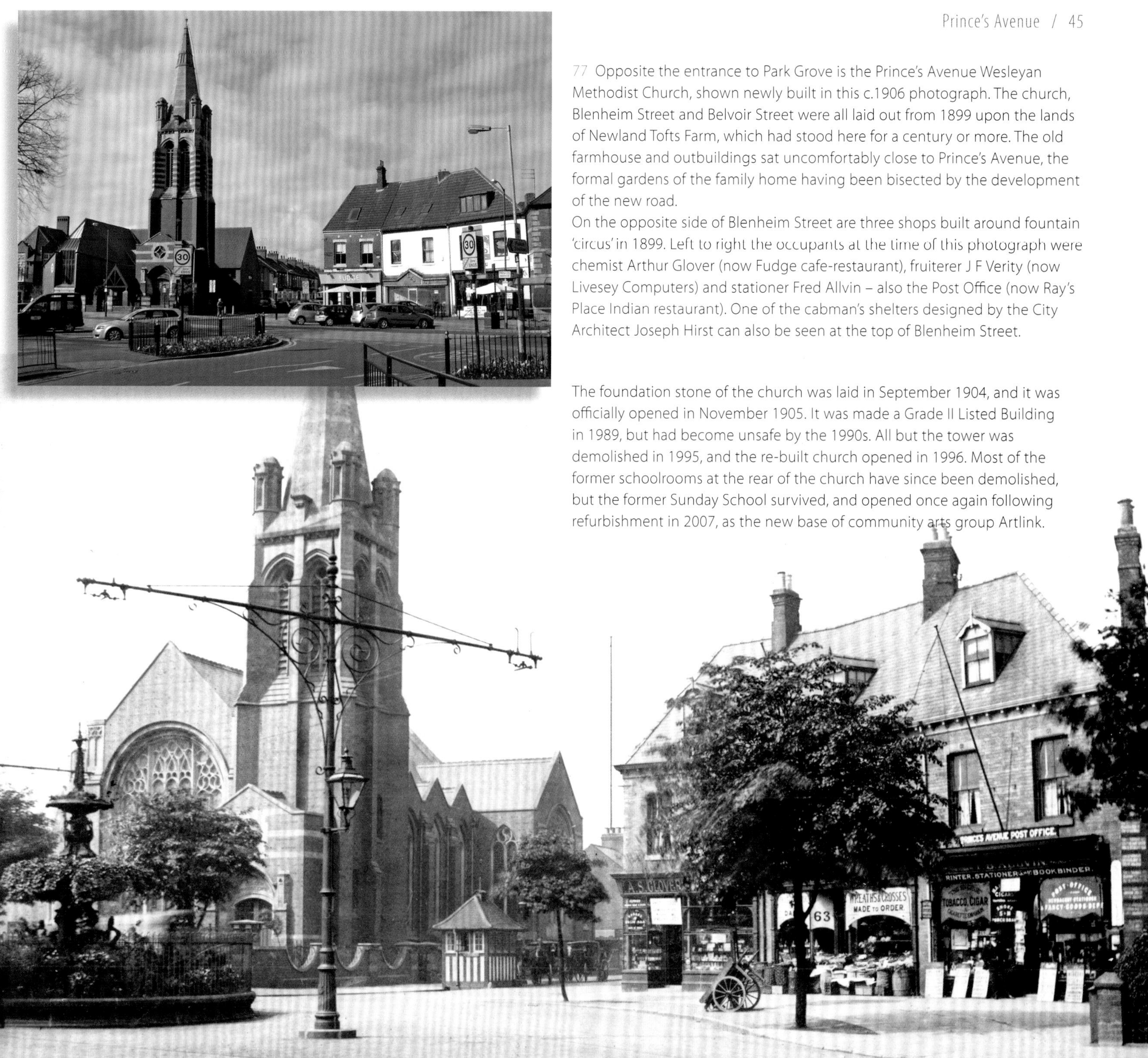

77 Opposite the entrance to Park Grove is the Prince's Avenue Wesleyan Methodist Church, shown newly built in this c.1906 photograph. The church, Blenheim Street and Belvoir Street were all laid out from 1899 upon the lands of Newland Tofts Farm, which had stood here for a century or more. The old farmhouse and outbuildings sat uncomfortably close to Prince's Avenue, the formal gardens of the family home having been bisected by the development of the new road.

On the opposite side of Blenheim Street are three shops built around fountain 'circus' in 1899. Left to right the occupants at the time of this photograph were chemist Arthur Glover (now Fudge cafe-restaurant), fruiterer J F Verity (now Livesey Computers) and stationer Fred Allvin – also the Post Office (now Ray's Place Indian restaurant). One of the cabman's shelters designed by the City Architect Joseph Hirst can also be seen at the top of Blenheim Street.

The foundation stone of the church was laid in September 1904, and it was officially opened in November 1905. It was made a Grade II Listed Building in 1989, but had become unsafe by the 1990s. All but the tower was demolished in 1995, and the re-built church opened in 1996. Most of the former schoolrooms at the rear of the church have since been demolished, but the former Sunday School survived, and opened once again following refurbishment in 2007, as the new base of community arts group Artlink.

78 & 79 (This page) The entrance to Park Grove can be seen on the right of this c.1903 photograph looking north along Prince's Avenue with a group of Edwardian girls promenading past the first of Prince's Avenue's two fountains. As is clear from the second photograph made around 1923, the fountains had become a hindrance to the increasing amount of traffic. Sadly, following problems fitting adequate lighting to the fountains, and despite letters of complaint to the council by locals, the fountains were removed in 1926.

80 & 81 (Next page) The terrace of shops between Park Grove and Hinderwell Street was constructed in 1897, probably as private houses. On the far right of this c.1905 photograph a garden fence and a bay window are still in place, suggesting a remaining private dwelling. Two shops in this block have retained their original trade for over a century; on the corner Joseph Wroe, a confectioner and dairyman ('Avenue Dairy') also ran an off-licence, which remains as 'The Off Licence' today (the smaller photograph shows the shop in the 1960s). Standing at the door of no.72 was butcher William Mawer, one of four butchers in Prince's Avenue in 1905. Long-standing butcher T L Norman continues the story in 2010.

The OFF LICENCE
FresHair
HINDERWELL STREET

A.CARTMELL
H.Y WILSON
& SON LTD
SAVILE HOUSE
WINE & SPIRIT
MERCHANTS
Beers & Stouts A.CARTMELL Wines & Spirits

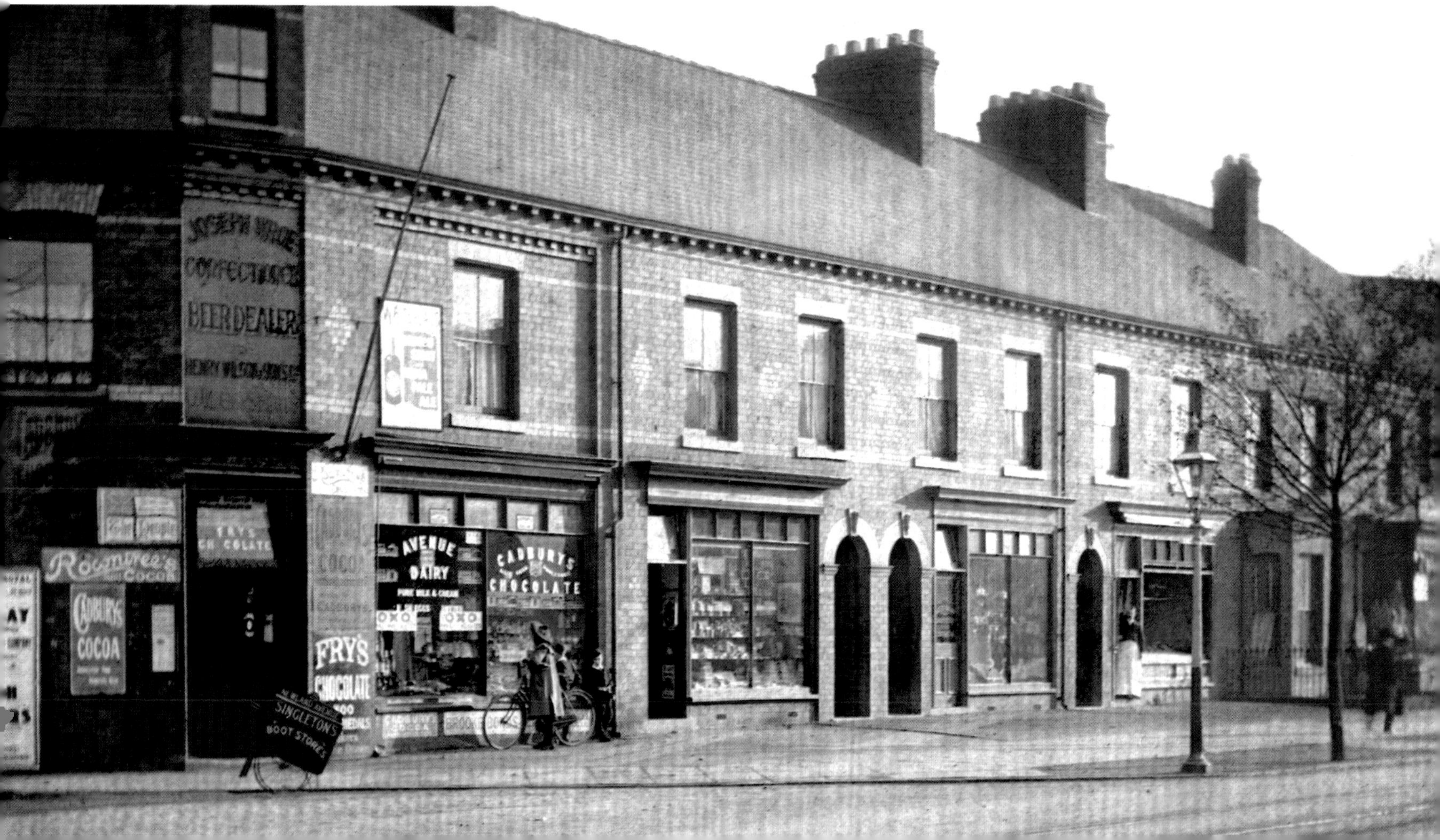

82 (Right) Hinderwell Street was developed by Colonel William Hall Wilkinson c.1880 and the north side of the street was noted as 'North Grove' in the early trade directories. Two other houses known as The Poplars lie at the east end of the street.

Hinderwell Street's modest appearance belies the fact that it forms part of a much older alignment. Houses on the north side of the street sit on a boundary important enough to be marked by a boundary stone at the side of what is now Prince's Avenue, shown on the 1853 and 1889 Ordnance Survey plans.

This was probably an old route for the dairy farmers of the Newland Tofts to the verdant meadows of 'Bull Fields' alongside the River Hull; the east end of this route marked by Park Lane and Stepney Lane. This old boundary also dictated the southern extent of Pearson Park.

83 (Left) On the far right of this photograph is Westbourne House, at the corner of Westbourne Avenue, which was demolished following the Second World War (see page 12).

The Avenues developer David Garbutt based his designs for the estate on the French style Boulevards, and at the opening of Prince's Avenue in 1875 revealed his plan to: 'continue the Boulevard from the Anlaby Road to the Cemetery gates'. The Boulevard had opened just a few years earlier, laid out with wide streets and a fountain.

His other great scheme, which also never came to fruition, was a 'boulevard from the end of Queen's Road to the east side of town', where he hoped some day to lay out an 'eastern estate'.

84 The same fountain, but looking north-west across Prince's Avenue from the Park entrance. In the background are some of the most distinctive houses on Prince's Avenue and some of the oldest – most dating from the late 1870s. The fountains in the Avenues were manufactured by King & Co of Hull and erected by 'Messrs Hebblethwaite, Son, and Bruce', and this one at least was in action during the opening ceremony of The Prince's Bank Avenue, as reported in the Hull and Lincolnshire Times 3rd April 1875: 'The band then struck up the National Anthem, and the fountain commenced playing'.
On the far left is a house that is actually part of Westbourne Avenue rather than Prince's Avenue, which explains its door at angle to the main road. The first resident here in the 1870s was Edward Dixon, who had cause to complain to the Cottingham Local Board in 1878 about Mr Garbutt's construction vehicles that were causing the roads to be 'cut up more than local traffic', and of 'the existence of stagnant water in the fountain opposite the Park entrance'. The fountains played infrequently, and were soon no more than elaborate plant holders.

85 & 86 By April 1861 work was still underway in the park and a report in the Hull Packet noted: 'The roads and paths excepting those close to the Princess Bank are cut out, and are undergoing the process of macadamization. The ground has been well levelled, some parts requiring to be raised and other parts lowered, and numerous mounds have been raised in accordance with the plan, giving the ground a very neat and tasteful appearance. Some of the mounds in the central part of the ground, have yet to be raised; and although the greater part of the trees, shrubs etc. are already in the ground, a considerable portion will have to be left over until next year. The drain on the north side of the park is all but completed and will fall into a sewer on the Beverley Road. The 'lake' is also cut out, but one of the two little islets which were to add to its appearance, is wanting. The bridge over the lake, the lodges, summer houses, drinking fountains and seats have of course to make their appearance, and will it is estimated be ready in little more than two months. Of the three trees planted at the fete last August, the centre one planted by Mr Pearson, and also one of the others, appears to have been affected by the weather, but the third is flourishing vigorously'.
The iron bridge can be seen in the 1910 photograph (left), and an octagonal bandstand erected in 1881 to the west of the lake, can be seen in the 1904 photograph below.

Plans for a park on this site were mooted in the Hull Packet in 1854: 'A public park has been hinted at from the Zoological Garden to the Cemetery, bounded by Newland Tofts Lane and the Cottingham Drain, but the lecturer feared its accomplishment was not very probable at present.'
It was not until August 1860 that progress was made with a 'colossal fete to commemorate the planting of the first tree', when 30,000 people visited Hull. The 27 acre site had been given by the then Mayor of Hull Zachariah Charles Pearson, who retained land on three sides of the park for his villa developments. Pearson is commemorated in the marble plaque erected in 1897 on a pillar of Cleveland ironstone, now a Grade II Listed Building.

87 & 88 Only one drinking fountain remains in Pearson Park (shown above right), donated by Henry John Atkinson in 1864. It was manufactured in cast iron by Watten, MacFarlane & Co of Glasgow at a cost of £32. Several other fountains were located in the park at various times, such as the one shown in the 1907 photograph (right). This was at the Beverley Road side of the park, close to where a cast iron urinal was also once situated. The fountain had originally stood in the Zoological Gardens off Spring Bank and was purchased at auction following the closure of the gardens in 1862.

The three fountains that still exist within the lake appear to have been in place since the park opened, and a second drinking fountain was located elsewhere in the park.

Top left is the statue of Queen Victoria by Thomas Earle, erected in 1863 and paid for by the mayor Mr Moss. In the background is one of many refreshment rooms and other buildings that once decorated the park.

89 (Left) The second of Pearson Park's Grade II Listed statues is that of Prince Albert, another work by sculptor Thomas Earle, erected in 1868. Behind the statue can be seen 'ruins from York Minster', which had been purchased for £18 at an auction of surplus goods following the closure of the Zoological Gardens in 1862. Later augmented by further stonework from Holy Trinity Church in Hull, all of the stonework was removed in the 1950s.

90 Only the Victorian Conservatory now survives from the original buildings laid in place by the park's designer James Niven, also curator of the old Botanic Gardens. The refreshment pavilion added in 1881 can be seen in this 1905 photograph, and whilst somewhat more stylish than today's model, it was no doubt less vandal-proof.

91 (Above) 20 of the 42 villa plots around the park had been sold by the time it opened in 1860, quickly recouping Mr Pearson the £7,800 he spent buying the land; the total sales eventually netting him £9,500. The laying out of the park, the making roads and the various planting cost £11,859, of which £7,502 was borrowed and about £4,300 came from public subscription. Despite the economy of the operation Mr Pearson found himself bankrupt for several other reasons by 1862.

92 The majority of the original villas survive but are now mostly converted to multiple occupation. Some have gone however, only to be replaced by rather austere modern dwellings, such as the 1970s apartment block shown above left.
Welwick House (left) designed by William Hagen in 1871 survives, but Willersley House, shown above, was one of the four convent houses demolished in 1975.

93 & 94 The park's main entrance gates were initially locked at night until residents complained of having to ring the gate-keeper to get in. The main entrance was originally intended to be nearer the corner of Queen's Road, hence the elaborate appearance of the cul-de-sac Eldon Grove, off the Beverley Road shown left in 1904. Other entrances were in Park Road, Park Lane and the Prince's Avenue gates. These were set back in 1875 when the circus was created around the fountain built there during the development of the Avenues estate. A small 'lodge' at the main Prince's Avenue entrance was built in 1863 and rebuilt in the 1890s as it appears today.
A further entrance for pedestrians was made from Prince's Avenue at the north-west corner in 1885. The ornate gates and 'triumphal arch' entrance from Pearson Avenue (seen here c.1905) were manufactured by ironmongers Young & Pool of Waltham Street in Hull. Made of cast iron and costing less than £450, sadly the gates and railings were removed during the second World War. Much of the other decoration has also gone, but the remaining structure was given Listed Building status in 1973, and partially restored in 1995.

3 • Newland Avenue & St John's Wood

96 Looking north along the Beverley Road, this 1904 photograph shows the entrance to Queen's Road on the left – all of the property on the left historically being in an area known as St John's Wood. In 1864 plans from a Mr Carlill were approved for three new streets to be called 'Alexander Road (sic), Queen's Road and Prince's Road, on land between the Beverley Road and Newlands Tofts Lane'; this was the start of the St John's Wood estate.

The Italianate building on the left was the Queen's Road Wesleyan Chapel built in 1878. The chapel closed following blitz damage and was used as a warehouse, whilst services continued in the school rooms (see page 57) until closure in 1967. Queen's House flats now occupy the site. At the side of the chapel is another of the Hirst designed cabman's shelters, and a drinking fountain donated by Mr Joseph Temple of Palmerston House, Chestnut Avenue. Mr Temple left £50 in his will for a fountain to be called after his name but the local board proposed a trough for horses. A compromise was reached with a drinking fountain for humans and small troughs for animals were built into the design. The fountain was removed to Pearson Park in 1925.

97 The school rooms of the Wesleyan chapel can be seen to the far right of this 1905 photograph, which looks west into Queen's Road. On the left is the iced over Cottingham Drain that ran open along the edge of the road until the 1960s, marking the southern boundary of St John's Wood. A Hull Packet article in December 1867 described the new development: 'St John's Wood immediately adjoins the Park, and is separated from the borough by the Park drain. St John's Wood consists of about 70 acres, and is bounded on the south by the Queen's-road, on the north by the Alexandra-road, on the east by the Beverley-road, and on the west by Temple Road [this appears to be an early reference to Newland Avenue]. Since 1864, when houses first began to make their appearance, eight new streets have been laid out, and plans of 107 houses have been approved by the Cottingham Local Board, and the habitations are now all built or in the course of erection. Nearly all the land has been sold by the original speculators, Messrs. J. Carlill and J. Story, and some choice lots have been re-sold at 50 per-cent advance. St John's Wood is most pleasantly and conveniently situated, and in view of the steady increase of house building, it is in contemplation to build a chapel and schools on the site, and thus place the district in this respect on a footing with Dairycoates and Beetonsville'.

98 & 99 The St John's Hotel was first named the Oddfellows Arms and opened c.1866 when beer seller Tyson Garner applied for his licence in that year. Maple Street, which runs alongside the pub, was originally named Argyle Street changing c.1887. The pub name was a reference to the Friendly Societies who may have held their meetings there. Following the development of St John's Wood and possibly also due to the fact that there had been another Oddfellows Arms in Hull since at least 1851 (in Osborne Street), the pub changed its name c.1890 to the more familiar St John's Hotel. The renaming may also have coincided with the pub being taken over by the Hull Brewery Co. Shown (right) outside the pub is 'Todgy' George William Green, a wagonette proprietor of Alexandra Road in the 1890s, in a photograph made by the then landlord.

Both Elm Street and Maple Street were intended to join with De Grey Street, but the construction of the high level railway line altered these plans. Both streets were demolished in 1981 and rebuilt with modern housing. With the exception of a few modern additions the St John's still retains its 1904-05 layout and rightly deserves its place as one of CAMRA's pub interiors of 'special heritage interest' in East Yorkshire.

100 In the shadows on the right of this 1905 photograph is the Cottingham Drain, with Elm Street corner to the left. Looking east along Queen's Road towards the Beverley Road, the image shows how the open drain defined the boundary of St John's Wood, which then lay in the parish of Cottingham. In September 1867 a report to the local board regarding the drainage of St John's Wood gave mixed messages: '... it is estimated that 305 [persons] occupy 86 houses in St John's Wood – seven new streets are already laid out; they are formed with cliff stone, and some of them covered with gravel. They are drained by means of 12 inch pipe drains and come together with the drainage from the village of Newland by means of open ditches into the Cottingham Drain – the sanitary condition of which they will most prejudicially effect. Some of the houses in St John's Wood are of a very slight description and have party walls four and a half inches thick and no back yards. The inhabitants of St John's Wood obtain their water from the Cottingham Drain which is contaminated as I have stated, but I am informed that steps are being taken to obtain a purer supply'. Thankfully the situation was relieved by December 1867 when another report noted improvements: 'not least by fixing a public pump to an artesian well made by Mr Speck of Hessle, and it is stated that the water is of excellent quality and equal to that derived from Springhead'.

101 & 102 A group of Roman Catholic buildings were constructed between Elm Street and Prince's Road in the early 20th Century, beginning with a school in 1903 with rooms above that were used as a chapel. The Sisters of Charity of St Vincent de Paul, who had been in Hull since the 1870s, founded St Vincent's Home for Boys at no.12 Wright Street in July 1890. In 1908 a new building was begun alongside the school and chapel in Queen's Road. Caring for orphan boys three to 14 years of age; the orphanage is shown here in photographs from c.1910. It closed c.1995 and has recently been converted to flats. In 1932-33 the present church of St Vincent was built to the designs of Hull architects Williams and Jopling. A more recent development in this block was the creation of St Vincent's Social Club c.1971 converted from three of the six houses that once stood in this short terrace. All of the Catholic developments here were overlooked by an older Anglican church that had stood for many years.

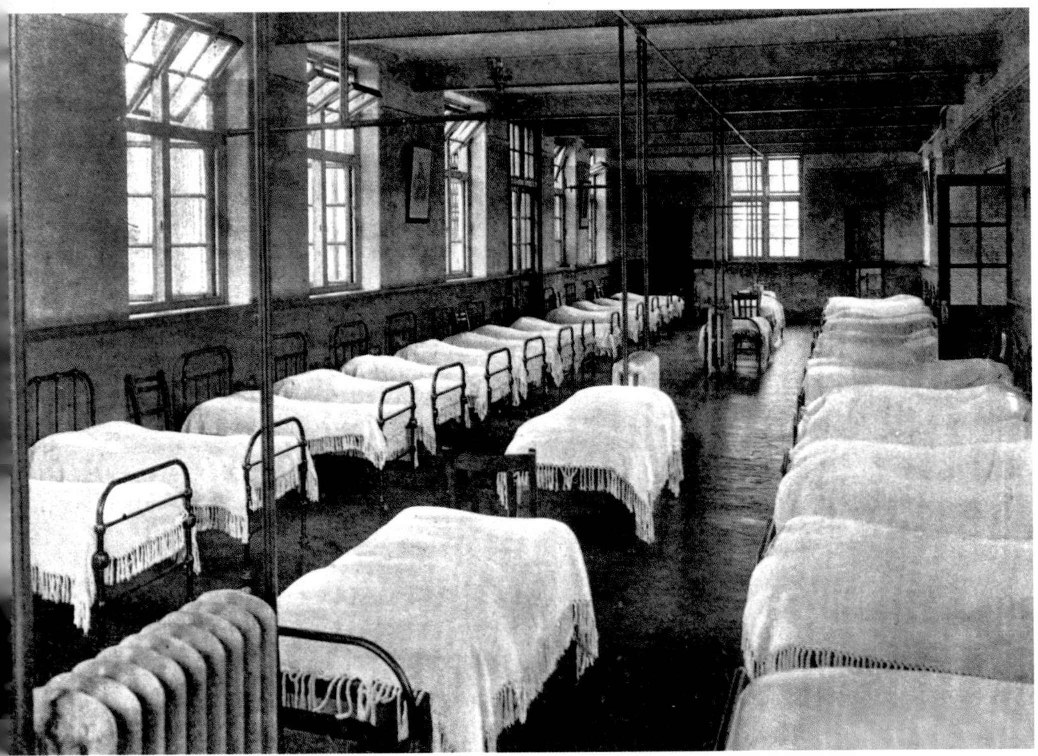

103 & 104 A temporary wooden church 'St Augustine of Hippo' was built in Queen's Road in 1884 to serve the rapidly growing suburb. By February 1884 a report noted that of the £1,154 raised by then, '£800 has been expended in land, and £380 in building a temporary church. About £80 is still needed to complete the church for fencing, furnishing, and other expenses. The work being then completed it is proposed in the course of another year, to erect the permanent Chancel at a cost of £1,000.'

It was not until 1892 that the church shown here was built to replace the temporary building. Designed by Temple Moore the church was demolished in 1976. The vicarage on the right and the former Parish Hall in Prince's Road (both built in 1902) survive.

The site of the church is now occupied by probation service accommodation, which also utilises the former vicarage, which it now adjoins.

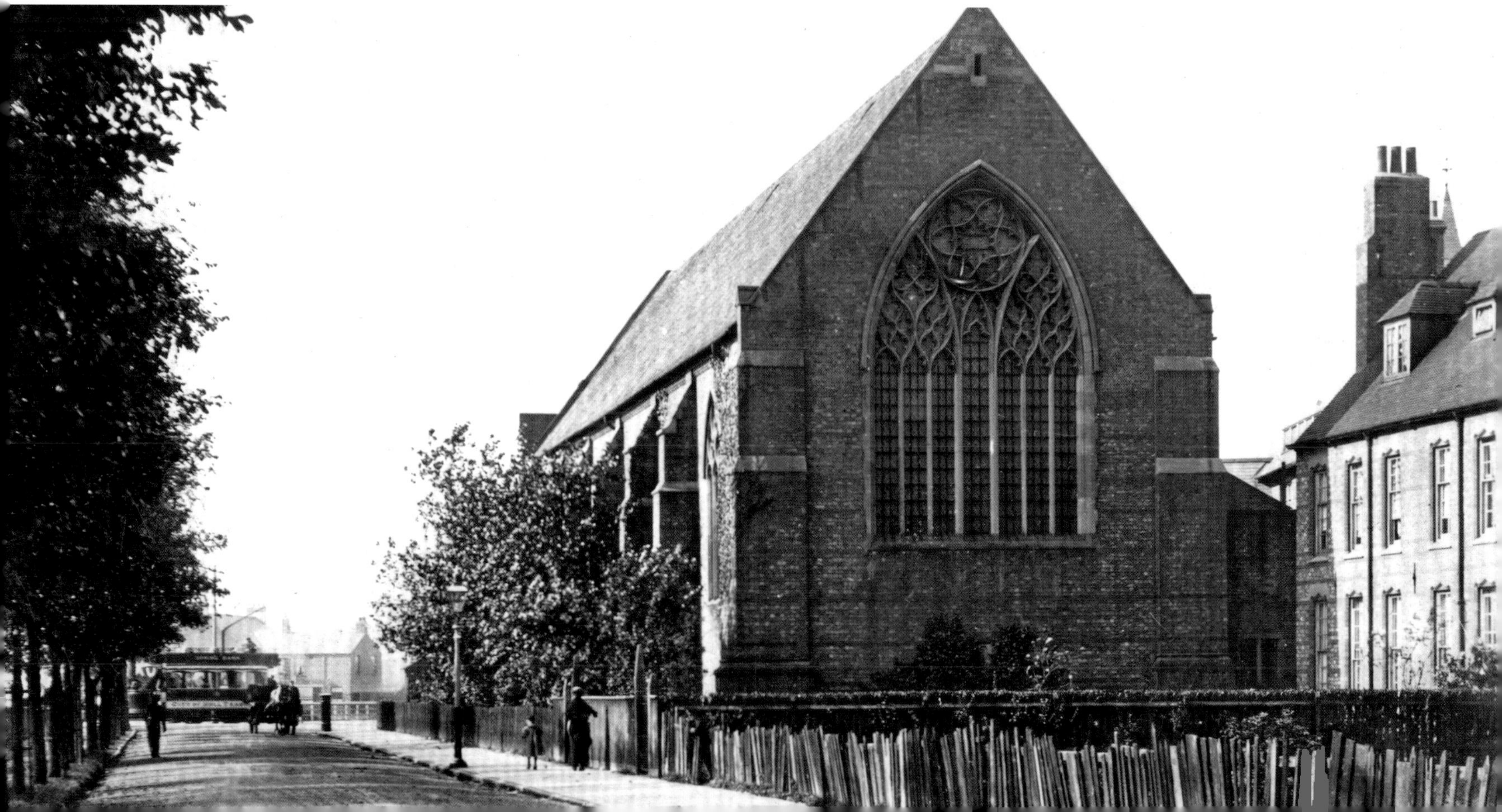

105 & 106 In August 1865 the Licensing Committee granted a licence to Mr W Purdon an auctioneer 'for a house intended to be called the Queen's Hotel, situated in the Queen's Road, near the Park'. The public house was duly opened in the newly laid-out Queen's Road that year, just one year before the St John's Hotel. The original building, probably built c.1863, has changed considerably inside and out, not least with the addition of a mansard roof in 1926. More recent alterations have resulted in the loss of individual rooms in the retail area, and in 2010 the frontage was refurbished to a high standard.

A bowling green was built in the 1890s and the Queen's had its own club, although the green was lost for the pub's car park in the 1960s. The photographs here show the pub in 1904 (right) and in the late 1950s with a web of trolley-bus wires overhead.

107 (Above) Mr Purdon, having established the Queen's Hotel, was keen to sell his new asset as well as the land he owned around it. In November 1866 he sold the pub and land; the natural boundary of his plot to the west defined the alignment of another new street in St John's Wood named Chestnut Avenue. The west end of Queen's Road is shown here in 1905 with the original bridge over the open Cottingham Drain visible on the right of picture.

108 Tenders were invited for the construction of Chestnut Avenue and other streets in the vicinity in May 1875, but its attraction was no doubt lessened by the Hull & Barnsley Railway's high-level line that cut across the area in the early 1880s on its way to the developing Alexandra Dock. By the time of the 1881 Census only 12 houses had been built in Chestnut Avenue. This view was made from Queen's Road in 1905.

109 Newland Avenue was laid out on the northern section of Newland Tofts Lane, just after the southern section had been developed as Prince's Avenue from 1874. Initially referred to as 'Newlands' or simply 'Tofts Lane', it was developed from the Cottingham Road end first. The whole of Newland Tofts Lane was often referred to as Mucky Peg Lane before its redevelopment, as travelling along it gave you 'mucky pegs' (legs) due to its boggy and often flooded nature.
The name Newland Avenue came into regular use in the early 1890s as the last of the Newland Tofts farmhouses were removed, suburban housing and small businesses having taken their place along the old agricultural lane.
A few of the properties shown in this 1904 photograph were built in 1889 but the majority date from the late 1890s. Looking north into Newland Avenue from the Queen's Road corner, at this date only a few of the houses had been converted to shops, including that of boot maker William Singleton, and a branch of 'Italian Warehousemen' J W Baker, on each corner of Ella Street seen on the left.

The majority of the houses seen here have been converted to shops, although some on the far left remain as private dwellings. Newland Avenue's cosmopolitan atmosphere has rarely been healthier than in 2010, and the area benefits from a very supportive local community and a traders association.

110 Ella Street was constructed c.1880 and was the first street to be laid out on the west side of Newland Tofts Lane. Initial development was restricted to the eastern end of the street as the west end was still open fields; development was restricted further by the curving alignment of the high-level railway line and its bridges, constructed from c.1882. Early newspaper accounts and trade directory references regarded Ella Street as part of St John's Wood, as the boundaries of the growing suburb were never quite clear. The view on the right looks west into Ella Street in 1904, with the entrances to some of its many terraces visible on either side.

111 The majority of the housing in Ella Street dates from the early 1900s, and this c.1912 view of the west end shows it complete except for a gap on the far right where the NER workers cottages would be built in 1925, 1926 and 1927. On the left, at the corner of Salisbury Street, is the grocer's shop of William Bass, more familiar as the premises of Jack Kaye from the late 1940s until closure some years ago. Kaye's old shop was demolished in January 2005, but his name lives on in nearby Jack Kaye Walk.

112 The 1880s railway bridge casts a shadow across this c.1906 photograph looking north along Newland Avenue. On the left are Reynoldson Street and Marshall Street, and on the right De Grey Street and Lambert Street. A pub for Newland Avenue was first suggested in 1877, when brewer Peter Robson of Waterworks Street applied for a licence for one he was proposing to build at the corner of Alexandra Road. His and many other applications over the next century were refused, although he was allowed an off-licence. It was not until June 1995 that the avenue had its first pub when the Hog's Head was created from the 1950s Teals furniture store at the corner of De Grey Street. This was latterly re-named the Nag's Head, one of many eating and drinking establishments in Newland Avenue's much changed street scene; it is just about to re-open as a pub having closed in 2009. In June 1995 there were two places to 'eat-in', one pub and a club in Newland Avenue – in April 2010 there are at least 16 venues to eat-in, a club and a newly renovated pub on the way.

113 (Left) No.122 Newland Avenue was converted from a private dwelling to a shop c.1908 and by 1915 grocer Arthur Hings was resident. Stiff competition next door at nos.118-120 in the shape of Wm Jackson's shop (opened in 1913) forced the small independent out. By the late 1920s no.122 had become one of Mallory's ironmonger's shops, and no.122 is now included within the enlarged Sainsburys at Jackson's store.

114 A different view of this section of the avenue – a terrace built in 1899, including the three-storey property at the corner of De Grey Street, now demolished. Heron Frozen Foods single-storey building now occupies this site, including the two former shops next door.

115 & 116 Reynoldson Street and Marshall Street were developed from 1897 by Thomas Reynoldson, one-time JP and director of the Kingston Gas Company, who married Jane Marshall, hence the adjoining street's name. In 1882 as the railway cut through his land, Mr Reynoldson took the railway company to court seeking damages for the effect the embankment and bridges had on the value of his land. After a poor result Mr Reynoldson's solicitor suggested the damage would render the land unlikely to be built upon for at least 30 to 50 years, but it was fully built upon within 20. Reynoldson Street is shown here in two photographs from 1905, looking east towards Newland Avenue and (below) looking west near the Marshall Street junction.

117 & 118 (Next page) Newland Avenue Board School was probably the first building to be built on Mr Reynoldson's land. Opened in 1896, it was reconstructed and extended in 1900, with accommodation for 320 boys, 320 girls, 210 juniors and 240 infants. It closed in 2005 and is now used by a variety of organisations.

These c.1905 views show school children posing in Marshall Street (above) and looking north across the playground in the larger view. The old school is now used partly as a Youth Club, and partly by various council services.

119 & 120 Plots of land between Beverley Road and Newland Tofts Lane were for sale in the local press from 1864, and De Grey Street was one of the first streets developed here from 1865. It was named after Viscount Goderich (born George Frederick Samuel Robinson) who was High Steward of Hull in 1863, and held the title of Earl De Grey & Ripon from 1859 to 1871. The photographs here date from 1905 and show the entrance from Newland Avenue (left) and looking from the Beverley Road end (below). On the right of the smaller picture can be seen the entrance to Chestnut Avenue.

On the left of the larger picture is Branch no.5 of the Hull Co-op, which opened in 1900 and closed in 1965. The boys with baskets may have been making local deliveries for the shop, which was latterly Don Law's motorcycle shop.

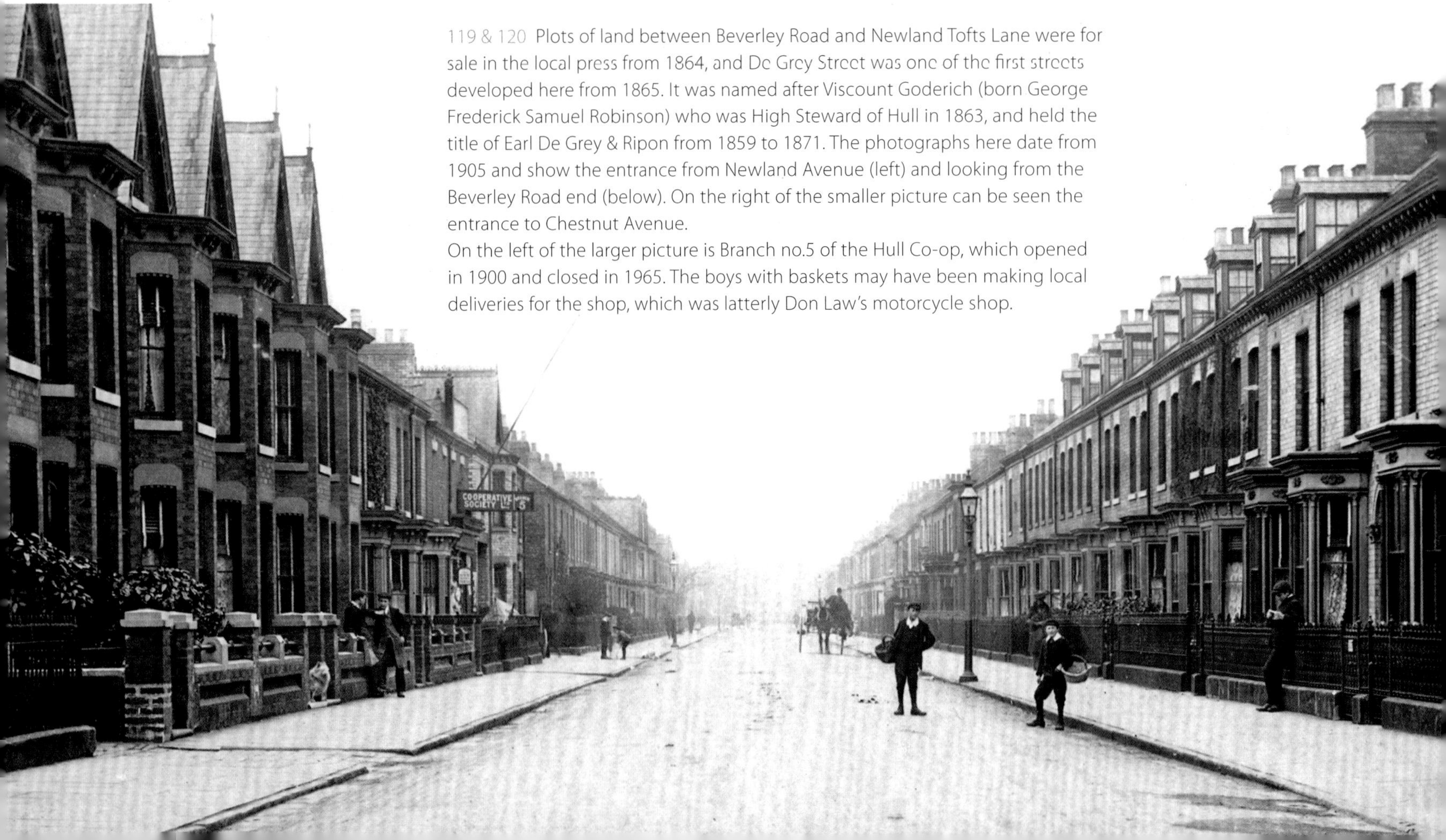

121 (Left) Albert Edward Buffey was a wholesale haberdasher and later a warehouseman based at no.71 De Grey Street from the late 1890s, and later including no.99. The business continued as Buffey & Sons until the 1970s, latterly at premises in Sharp Street. His horse-drawn van is shown here c.1910.

122 At no.96 De Grey Street was grocer William Tindale, whose shop was also numbered 55 Prince's Road. Prince's Road was also laid from c.1865, a decade earlier than Prince's Avenue, although very few properties were actually built until the late 1870s onwards. Tindale remained from c.1904 until the 1920s, and more recently this was an antique shop, but is now a unisex hair salon known as Wild Cherry.

123 Probably named after Princess Alexandra, who married the Prince of Wales in 1864, Alexandra Road marks the northern extent of the St John's Wood development. It is another of the earliest roads in the area, laid-out from c.1866 but developing slowly, and less than half built upon by 1890. It is shown here looking west from the Beverley Road end c.1905.

The kink in the building line on the right, where three shops project out, marks the point at which two old field boundaries met, their hedges still defining property lines centuries after their passing. Sharp Street was laid out here from 1886 (see page 74).

124 This c.1910 photograph shows Newland Avenue looking south towards the railway bridge, from the entrance to Edgecumbe Street. On the left of the picture, the block with a decorative tower (built c.1903) marks the bold entrance to Lambert Street. Thankfully Newland Avenue retains many small independent traders who are well supported by locals.

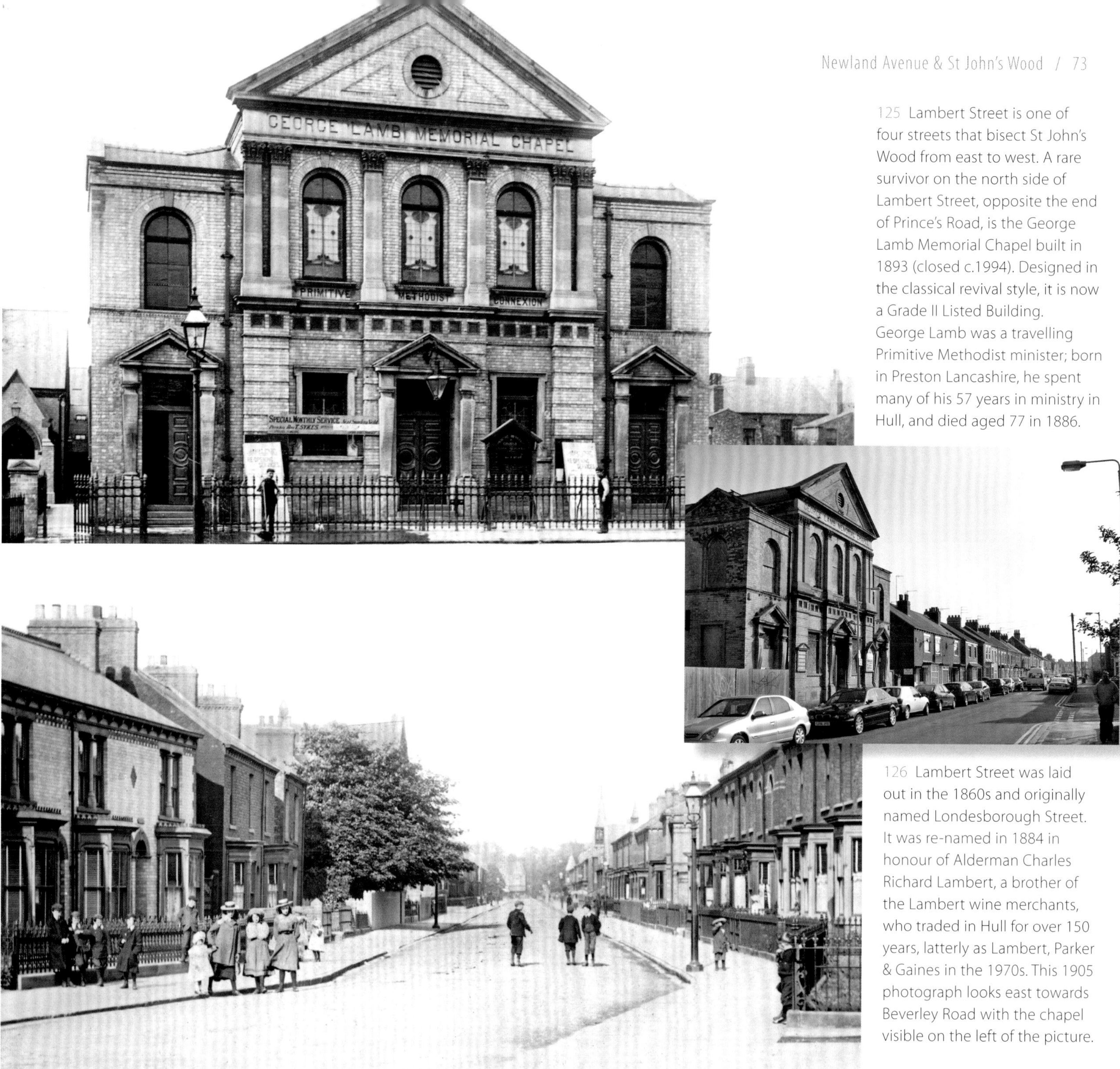

125 Lambert Street is one of four streets that bisect St John's Wood from east to west. A rare survivor on the north side of Lambert Street, opposite the end of Prince's Road, is the George Lamb Memorial Chapel built in 1893 (closed c.1994). Designed in the classical revival style, it is now a Grade II Listed Building. George Lamb was a travelling Primitive Methodist minister; born in Preston Lancashire, he spent many of his 57 years in ministry in Hull, and died aged 77 in 1886.

126 Lambert Street was laid out in the 1860s and originally named Londesborough Street. It was re-named in 1884 in honour of Alderman Charles Richard Lambert, a brother of the Lambert wine merchants, who traded in Hull for over 150 years, latterly as Lambert, Parker & Gaines in the 1970s. This 1905 photograph looks east towards Beverley Road with the chapel visible on the left of the picture.

127 & 128 Land on the west side of Newland Avenue was developed much later than that on the east. The east side – Grafton Street, Lambert Street and De Grey Street, were developed as part of St John's Wood from the early 1860s. The streets on the west side – Lambton, Raglan, Ventnor etc., were developed from the late 1890s onwards with the exceptions of Ella Street (see page 65) and Sharp Street – shown below c.1906. Named after J Fox Sharp (a property developer and surveyor to the local board of health), it was laid out from 1886 on land north of Robert Freeman's brick & tile works; the bricks made here would no doubt have been used to build many of the houses in this area. The later houses, set back slightly on both sides of the street, were built upon the brick yard and the brick ponds formed during the extraction of the clay. The Prince's Bank Brick & Tile Works (established c.1878) closed c.1894, and the houses were built on the site by 1896. Shown left is a view of Raglan Street as seen from Newland Avenue c.1904, before Exmouth Street was laid out from 1907. The creation of the new street enabled Raglan Street to be extended further west.

Sharp Street remains almost intact, a long street of housing of varying quality. A new development at the Newland Avenue end is the Newland Shopping Arcade, which lies on a site originally occupied by the 'Star Laundry & Carpet Shaking Works', established in 1888, closing in the early 1920s.

129 The 1881 Census recorded just 36 houses dotted along 'Newland Tofts Lane', and a further ten houses in Walter's Terrace that were built in 1877. Walter's Terrace was the first terrace built off the north east side of Newland Tofts Lane (to the right of these pictures), and a sale notice from April 1877 described them as: 'All those nine dwelling houses being the southern half of a new terrace called Walter's-terrace, each house containing good sized shop, sitting room, kitchen, three bedrooms, yard and out-offices. The above lots have recently been built in a very substantial manner, and are situated in a rapidly improving neighbourhood'. Also for sale was the house and shop adjoining the terrace on 'Newland Tofts Road'.

The 1877 houses still exist on the south side of Walter's Terrace, but the north side was demolished in 1981. This c.1914 photograph shows the area, with Walter's Terrace just off the picture. Most of the houses here were constructed in the late 1870s, whereas the houses on the west side were constructed between 1905 and 1908. On the far left, the corner of Ventnor Street was butcher Harold Brown, no.215 Newland Avenue, which remained a butchers' until the 1970s. All but one of these houses remain residential in 2010.

130 No.197 Newland Avenue was built c.1907 as part of matching terraces that stretch from Sidmouth Street to the far side of Ventnor Street. A purpose–built shop was built on the corner of each block, with accommodation above. The first resident of no.197, on the corner of Torrington Street, was draper William Smith whose business remained here until the Second World War. 'Smith's Fent & Drapery Stores', as they became known, had further branches in Spring Bank and the Beverley Road. Fent was a term used for surplus material, which was often the excess at the end of a roll after a production run in a mill.
Since the 1990s no.197 has been the premises of the Newland Bedding Centre, retaining a vague drapery theme throughout. The shop is shown here around 1920 and in 2010.

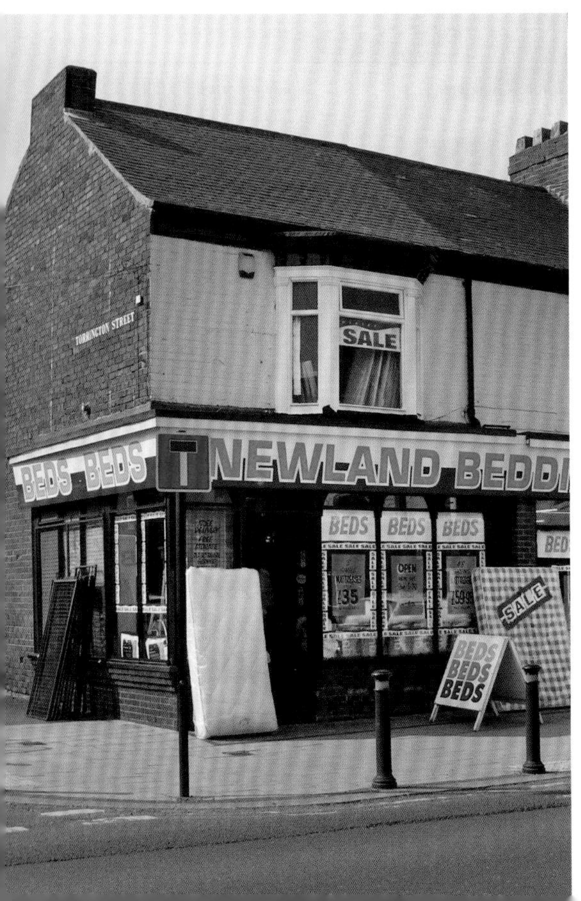

131 This 1911 photograph shows no.208 Newland Avenue, almost opposite Smith's Fent Stores, decorated to celebrate the coronation of King George V in that year. Alfred Oyston, also a butcher, was the first occupant of no.208 in the early 1880s. The shop, and those adjoining, had been built c.1877 – probably in the same development as Walter's Terrace (see page 75). By 1904 William Vickerman had taken over the shop and his premises were also a registered slaughterhouse. By 1936 Mrs Mary Vickerman was listed as a butcher at no.208 and by 1939 the shop was empty. In the early 1940s butcher T H Smithson occupied the building, remaining until the 1960s when there were still at least seven butchers in Newland Avenue – another shop retaining its original trade for almost a century. Latterly T Batty (Builders) Ltd (since 1995), it is now the office of an accommodation agent known as Unicom.

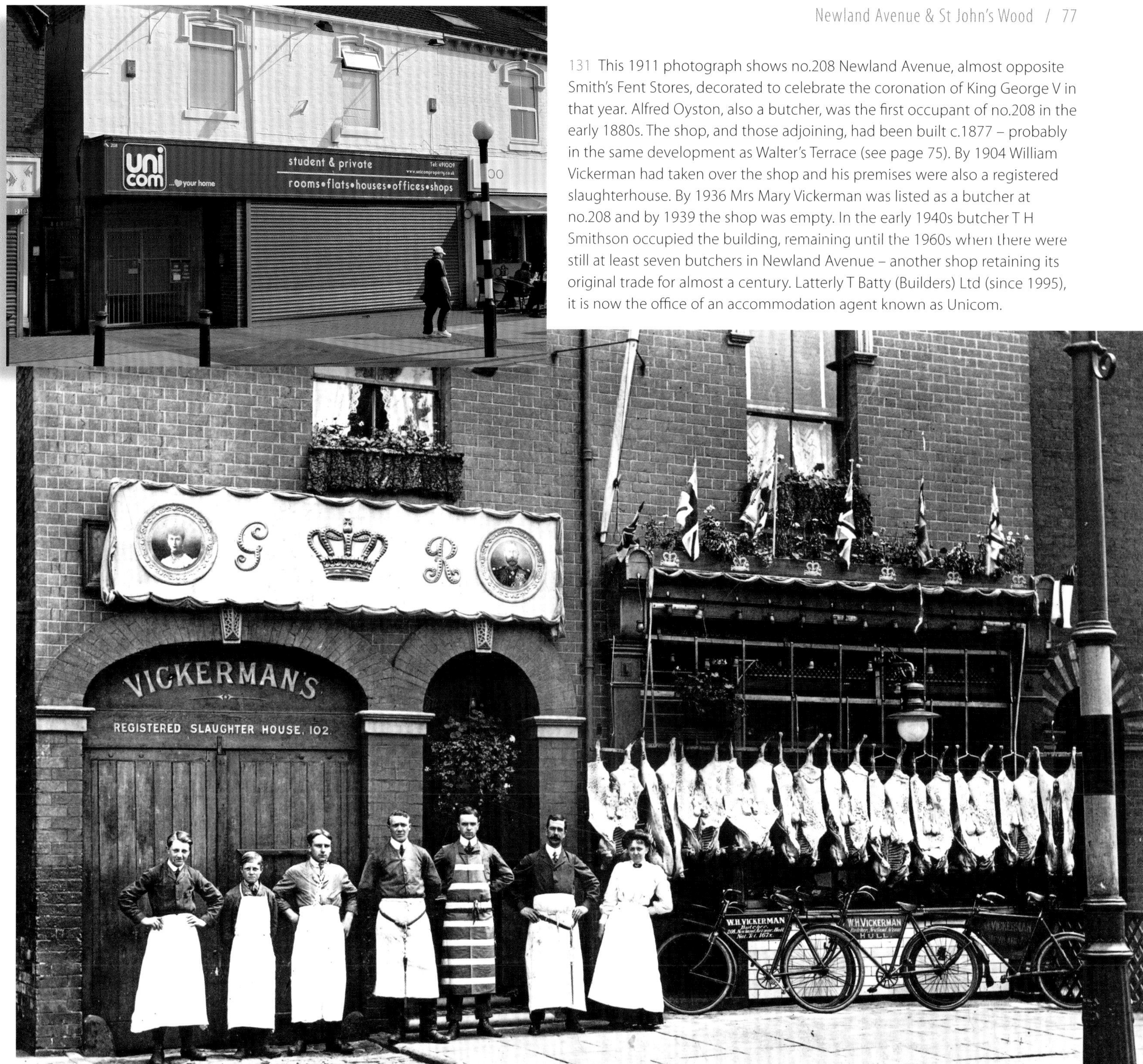

132 This shop was built as part of the terrace between Torrington Street and Ventnor Street around 1904, originally as a private house. Most of these properties remained private dwellings until c.1920, when many were converted to small shops and businesses.
Robert Gray Searby's 'High Class Groceries & Provisions' store was probably the first business to occupy the converted dwelling shown here, and served the Newland Avenue shoppers throughout the 1920s. From the 1930s it was a tailor's shop and then returned to private occupation. A more recent change of use has seen the old shop change from retail premises to an eat-in or takeaway Italian food outlet in 2009. 'La Delizia' is shown above in April 2010.

133 Newland Avenue as we know it, was developed from the Cottingham Road end and the junction can be seen in this photograph. The open space on the left of the c.1904 view further illustrates how the east side of Newland Avenue was developed much earlier than the west. Most of the buildings on the right (east) side of the picture date from the late 1870s, whereas the left (west) side had yet to be built upon with the Ventnor Street, Walgrave Street and the terraces in between.

The ornate pole on the right is a sign that Newland Avenue had been on the electric tram route since January 1903, when Route 'S' was extended from its previous terminus at Queen's Road. A circular service also ran along Newland Avenue from 1919 to 1923, and the Route 'SC' ran via Prince's Avenue and Newland Avenue as far as Newland Park from 1919 to 1923. On either side of the entrance to Newland Avenue were two important religious buildings, both of which can be seen in the picture.

134 The Newland Wesleyan Chapel, on the corner of Newland Tofts Lane and Cottingham Road, opened in March 1858. Designed by William Botterill it cost £600 including the land. The chapel had seating for 200, and a Sunday School that held 70 children. Closing in 1900 when a new chapel was built opposite, it was used by the Port of Hull Society until demolition in 1966. A German Lutheran church of 1968 was on the site until 2006, when the Hull Community Church was built here.

135 The new chapel that was built opposite the 1858 building, was the Newland Wesleyan School Chapel, built in 1901 to the designs of architects Gelder & Kitchen. Costing £7,700 the school initially had seating for 850. A new church building was built alongside in 1928 facing the Cottingham Road, which remains in use today as the Trinity Methodist Church. The old chapel and nearby Sunday School have been completely demolished and the site is now used as a car park, serving the later buildings.

4 • Newland & the Cottingham Road

137 Newland, once a hamlet within the parish of Cottingham, is now usually accepted to be an area that runs roughly from the north end of Chanterlands Avenue (originally known as Far Salt Ings Lane at this end) to just east of the Beverley Road. South of this historically was 'Newland Fields' upon which St John's Wood was later built, and Newland Tofts – the site for the Avenues estate and later Newland Avenue itself. Newland is mentioned in land records dating from the 12th Century, when an ancient stream named Mill Beck ran through Cottingham and Newland to the River Hull at Hull Bank. A track or lane had probably linked Cottingham to the old ferry at Stoneferry since that time but is only mentioned with certainty in 1450 when money was bequeathed for its repair. This 'Cottingham Road' was the only direct link from Hull to Cottingham via Newland until the 20th Century. Newland is now part of Hull following several extensions of the city boundary from 1882, prior to which everything north of the Cottingham Drain (the south side of Queen's Road) was within the parish of Cottingham. The Newland Park estate was developed by engineer Robert Aspland Marillier who lived in the newly developed Prince's Avenue at that time. Laid out in 1877-78, the roads in Newland Park were finished by 1878 according to the local press, and tenders for several contracts were invited in the Hull Packet during 1878 – each for 'pairs of villas in Newland Park'. Many of the contracts were given by architect William Botterill, who designed some of the original houses, including the first – Brookside, of 1878 – the large pair of semi-detached houses shown above. Initially sales were few, and ten years after the estate was laid out only six of the 90-plus large plots had been built upon. By the turn of the Century there were just seven houses, but by 1910 the figure had reached 30, and by 1926 there were over 100 occupied houses. The c.1905 image above shows the Cottingham Drain running south within the estate. Looking north across the main estate road, it is no longer possible to make this view, as the land in the foreground is now fully built upon. Nos.151 and 153 on the far left survive.

138 & 139 (Next page) The main picture shows Welham Lodge, built for grinding mill owner Robert Collingham c.1880, and is one of only three surviving houses from the original six. Shown here c.1905, it has undergone very little change. The slightly younger no.44 Newland Park is shown in the smaller photographs; dating from the turn of the last century it too has undergone few changes in the last 100 years, and is shown here c.1910.

140 In stark contrast to the piecemeal development of Newland Park, the 20th Century developments at the west end of the Cottingham Road were typical of the new mass-production era. Newland Park had been a speculative development of houses, mostly built to order for fairly wealthy clients, but houses such as these in Fairfax Avenue (built in 1931) supplied a healthy demand for new ready-built suburban housing.

141 The Cottingham Road remained a rural lane until the 1920s, when it was widened, given extended tram routes, and a new pub. The Good Fellowship Inn opened in 1928 at the corner of Near Salt Ings Lane, another old agricultural track redeveloped as Kenilworth Avenue c.1934. This was the scene looking east at that time with the Newland Beck still running open on the right.

142 & 143 Hull's early 1920s council housing estates are recognisable by the neo-Georgian style of the local amenities, such as these. This development began with Bentley Grove and Tickton Grove in 1925, leading off the north side of the Cottingham Road via Cottingham Grove; the Quadrant was built later, in 1929.

Hull faced a housing shortage after the First World War but and three new estates were begun boosted by subsidies from Housing Acts from 1920 to 1935. The majority of the new builds were to re-house those displaced by the demolition of poor quality housing in the city centre, a process begun c.1900. The shops shown here c.1930, are at the southern extent of the North Hull Estate, and remain mostly occupied in 2010.

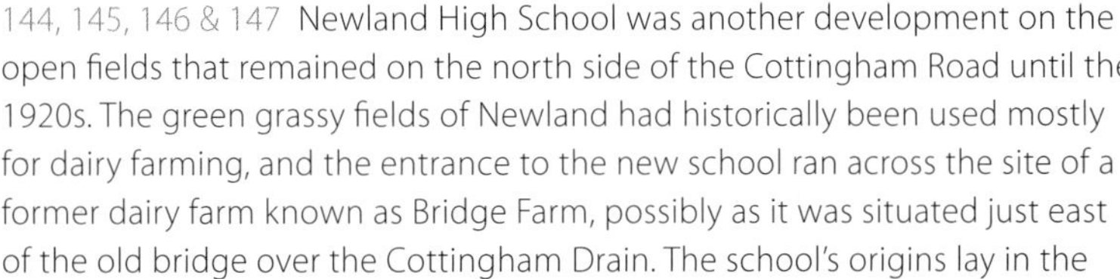

144, 145, 146 & 147 Newland High School was another development on the open fields that remained on the north side of the Cottingham Road until the 1920s. The green grassy fields of Newland had historically been used mostly for dairy farming, and the entrance to the new school ran across the site of a former dairy farm known as Bridge Farm, possibly as it was situated just east of the old bridge over the Cottingham Drain. The school's origins lay in the Brunswick Avenue Central Secondary School, which became a girls school in 1907; it was this school that transferred to this newly constructed facility in 1920, when it was re-named Newland High School for Girls. In 1936 there were 598 pupils and by 1963 there were 680. The aerial view dates from the 1950s and the photographs of the gymnasium, dining room and lecture room date from the 1920s; 90 years later Newland Girls School is as successful as ever.

148 & 149 Further educational facilities were built adjoining the Newland High School from 1925-28. The City of Hull Municipal Training College buildings were built in 1925, one of which is shown on the right, the others visible on the far left of the later photograph below. Newland High School is also visible directly north of the new buildings.
The aerial view shows the first two Hull University buildings constructed in 1927-28; the Arts & Administration building (now the Venn Building) on the left, and Science (now the Cohen Building), Library and Common Rooms on the right. Further land was bought for future expansion by the forward thinking university development team, headed by Thomas Ferens, as development either side was almost impossible. This c.1930 photograph shows the full extent of the university lands at that time.

150 The boundary of Hull has shifted several times bringing land and often small hamlets within the municipal borough. The effects of these extensions were felt in Newland in the changes made in 1882, and more especially in 1897. Until that time only the south side of the Cottingham Road was built upon, the north remaining open fields save for the occasional dairy farm building. It was not just educational buildings and housing that filled the former grassland however, as from the late 19th Century grand homes, once reserved to the south side of the Cottingham Road, began to be constructed on the north side.

Shown below is St Michael's Mount – Newland, built c.1908 on the north side of what is now called Inglemire Avenue. The house would have enjoyed uninterrupted views from its balcony, looking back towards the Cottingham Road, until the housing developments of the early 20th Century. The house was demolished in the 1980s, and the flats shown here, retaining the name St Michael's Mount, were constructed on the site.

151 (Above) New streets and terraces were built from 1897 on the north side of the Cottingham Road. Mostly spreading west from the Beverley Road junction, where the compulsory purchase of many old properties took place in 1907. Cranbrook Avenue, shown here still under construction in 1909, was one such development. This area is now popular for student accommodation, which is clear by the large amount of letting agents in the vicinity.

152 (Below) Developments south of the Cottingham Road are in the main much older than those on the north. Falmouth Street is an exception, and was also built c.1909. Shown here just after opening is the shop of tobacconist and confectioner Walter Cullen, at the junction with the Cottingham Road. This was also a Post Office until at least the 1980s, but is now a branch of a letting agent known as Kexgill, who specialise in student accommodation.

153 It is often difficult to accept the huge changes that have taken place in our streets, and this change is often more pronounced in suburban areas. This tranquil 1904 view of the Cottingham Road could hardly be more different from the scene in 2010. Looking west, with the entrance to Newland Avenue on the left, the road had yet to be widened at this date, and on the left the Newland Beck still ran open. The Cottingham Beck, created on the line of an ancient stream, became 'Newland Beck' as it entered the Newland area on its journey west to its out-fall into the River Hull at Stoneferry. This was the heart of the old hamlet of Newland and records of property in this area date from as early as the 12th Century, and by 1672 there were at least 30 households. Land in the Newland area was drained under the Enclosure Act of 1766, which led to the creation of the many drains and dykes that still flow across Hull to this day. One of these, the Cottingham Drain of 1771, runs (culverted) across the Cottingham Road into Newland Park (see page 82) and two more cross Clough Road – the Beverley & Skidby Drain and the Beverley & Barmston Drain.

154 (Left) Leonard Smales was standing at the gate of his home – the White House Farm, in this c.1905 photograph. His was one of very few buildings that were situated on the north side of the Cottingham Road prior to the early 1900s, and would have been on the far right of picture 153 on the previous page.
Mr Smales had been a cow-keeper and dairyman at this address since the 1890s, although the property obviously dates from the 18th Century or earlier. The White House Farm was compulsory purchased in 1908 and cleared for re-development. The demolition of the old farm was required for the construction of additional buildings–a laundry, recreation buildings, and a second lodge, for the Port of Hull Society's Sailors' Orphan Homes, subsequently Newland Homes.

155 (Right) The society was founded in 1821 at the St Mary's Boys Schoolroom in Salthouse Lane. Other small rooms were found in Waterhouse Lane (1842), Castle Row (1862) and Spencer Street, providing accommodation for children who could not be cared for in their own homes. In 1867 donation of £5,000 from Titus Salt, a Bradford mill owner and philanthropist, enabled the purchase of Thanet House in Park Street, now better known as a Hull College building. However, the society's annual report for 1893 noted: We have reached the limit of our accommodation in Park Street.
This consideration, and the increasing number of children seeking admission has decided the Committee to take a further step. A plot of ground of six acres has been purchased, with the option of a further quantity, upon which it is intended to erect a Cottage Home Colony.
The Newland site was opened on 6th June 1895 and Thanet House in Park Street was sold to the municipal education authority in 1897.

156, 157 & 158 Daily life at Newland Homes is shown in these photographs dating from the early 1900s. The character of the service the society provided was to educate and train orphan children of naval or merchant seamen, fishermen and river-men and provide support for their families. The society also acted as agents for the Shipwrecked Mariners Society, and by the 1930s there were 250 children in the various houses on the site. The first to open was 'Hannah Pickard Home', and most of those that followed also bore the name of other benefactors; by 1907 all of the 10 homes were complete. A bandstand was built with donations from friends in Grimsby, and in 1921 swimming baths and a new laundry were added with donations from T R Ferens.

159, 160 & 161 In more recent years changes in policy led to a decline in residential child care referrals, mostly from the late 1990s. At this point the trustees decided to sell the Newland Homes estate. St Nicholas School (of 1897), located within the grounds, was transferred to the local council, minimising the effect on the school children. The rest of the site was eventually sold off in 2009, and current plans are for the Grade II Listed Buildings to be converted to student accommodation, with a scheme to build around 40 extra houses and to demolish some buildings.
The Sailors Families Society continues to help relatives of seafarers, now working mostly within the homes of those in need.

162 & 163 (Left) Amongst the oldest buildings on the south side of the Cottingham Road is the Gardeners' Arms pub. Originally a market gardener's home, it became a beer-house c.1851, although the building appears to date from the 18th Century. The pub has been altered several times, but is likely to contain remnants of the original single-storey house. Shown bottom left c.1870, and in the 1960s in the centre photograph, the Gardener's is now an established venue with the huge student population of the Newland area.

164 (Below) In 1909 a new tram car depot opened across the road from the Gardener's Arms, squeezed on a long irregular plot east of the Newland Homes. Land for the new tram shed was purchased in 1902 but development was delayed, the new depot eventually taking all cars that had previously been kept at Stepney Lane when it opened in 1909.

165 The Spring Bank - Queens Road tram route was extended to serve Newland Avenue from 1903, terminating at the Cottingham Road junction. In 1919 a circular service was introduced where trams running clockwise via Newland Avenue and the Beverley Road had the letter S, whilst cars operating anti-clockwise had the letter B. Another route (BC), also introduced in 1919, was extended to the Good Fellowship Inn in 1925 and ran from the city via the Beverley Road, and the Cottingham Road to Newland Park. This was supplemented by the SC route, which ran via Newland Avenue and the Cottingham Road. The circular routes and the SC ceased in December 1923; from that time the S ran to Newland Avenue and the Cottingham Road, and the B to Newland via the Beverley Road. Trams on the Cottingham Road route to Hall Road, and Newland Avenue, all ceased in July 1934.

The main shed, shown here c.1910, was extended in 1925 and demolished in the 1990s. Only the much-changed office block on the left remains, known as Larrard House. This is now used as a letting agency, at the entrance to a small 1990s housing estate named The Trees

166 (Right) The 61 trolley-bus was passing the old Waddington's building in this 1961 photograph. Latterly MCA Waddington, this was probably the last of the Cottingham Road's original industrial buildings and was demolished in 1982. Waddington's had been here since c.1845, although a tanner was recorded in Newland as early as 1752, as well as brick-yards, roperies and at least one mill.

167 (Below) The Newland Homes fence can just be seen on the left of this c.1905 photograph, alongside a gap where the new tram depot was to be built. Again, this image clearly shows the extent to which the Cottingham Road was widened – the new houses on the left set back from the line of the old lane. These houses were soon to become shops, as the pictures on the following page show.

168 No sooner had the terraced housing been built adjacent to the old Haworth Arms, than it was being converted to retail premises. Picture 167 on the previous page shows the new houses shortly after construction, with just a few converted as shops, and most retaining their small front gardens and railings. But by the time of the c.1920 view below all of the houses but one had lost their garden and gained a shop-front; the exception being the premises of a carting agent whose works were at the rear, and whose arched entrance still survives today.

The first 'shops' in the Cottingham Road were boot-makers Balme & Co and a Post Office, both situated in the very old buildings attached to the Haworth arms, which can be seen in the distance in both photographs (it was rebuilt in 1927). More traditional shops followed in the new century, when confectioner Annie Sturdy and the 'Post Office Savings Bank and Stationery' shop of Mrs Martha J Taylor were the first in the block c.1904. By the time of the c.1920 photograph just one awning has the wording 'Cafe' imprinted upon it. In 2010 the Cottingham Road has a number of cafe-bars, following the trend set in Prince's Avenue and increasingly Newland Avenue, adding further attraction to this popular student neighbourhood.

169 (Right) A Beverley Road tram at the Newland terminus on the Beverley Road corner, decorated for the coronation of King George V in 1911. In the background is the wall of 'Newland Grove', the home of Avison Terry, a philanthropic businessman, and Mayor of Hull in 1827 and 1829. His was one of several grand houses in Newland (see page 99).

170 (Below) Newland's main period of growth followed the turn–piking of the Cottingham Road in 1764, and the early 19th Century development was restricted to the area around the toll bar at the Beverley Road junction. By the 1850s development had spread predominantly west (as far as the Cottingham Drain), as wealthy Hull businessmen built more homes in the leafy suburbs, far away from the cramped, polluted and increasingly smelly city.

Four of the fine houses (nos.25 to 31), built by well-to-do merchants and businessmen in the 19th Century, survive at this point on the Cottingham Road. Some can be seen on the right (south side) of this 1905 photograph looking east, one now home to a Chinese restaurant.

171 (Above) St John's Newland is shown here in a 1904 view that can no longer be made, as shops built along the Beverley Road now fill the foreground. The church was built in 1833 (architect William Hutchinson), due mostly to the efforts of Avison Terry who lived opposite, and raised £1,000 of the total building costs of around £1,650. The church was added to in 1893 and 1902, and a parsonage built in 1863, also survives.

172 (Below) Avison Terry (1774-1866) lived at Newland Grove from c.1803, and this photograph shows it, possibly with later additions, c.1905. Prior to the construction of the chapel at Newland Avenue in 1858, the 'Barn Preaching House' was located in Avison Terry's grounds. Grove House as it became known, remained a private residence until c.1913 when it was used as a Nurses' Home annexed to the Sculcoates Union Workhouse. The house was demolished in 1926 as this junction was improved, and the site was used as a fire station during the war. The Grove House residential care homes, built in 2004, now occupy the site.

173 (Right) Clough Cottages, seen here in the 1930s, were situated on the north side of Clough Road, and still within 'Newland'. These 18th Century dwellings were probably brick-makers houses, as they were close to brick yards that stood in this area until the 20th Century. The photograph was made by the Corporation Health Department shortly before their demolition.

174 Minton Street was part of a small development on the south side of Clough Road, built from c.1907 adjoining the grounds of Newland Grove at the corner of the Beverley Road. The new housing extended east to the much older Worthing Street that was laid out as the northern extent of St Leonard's Road c.1880, development having been cut-short when the high-level railway cut across c.1885. Brooklyn Street and Vermont Street, on the east side of the Beverley Road were also laid out on part of the Newland Grove grounds in the 1890s. Seen here during a First World War Peace Party, all of these houses in Minton Street survive in 2010.

5 • The Road to Stoneferry

176 The route north from the old town of Hull to the hamlets and villages of Stoneferry, Sutton and Wawne was historically a circuitous one along the High Road to Sutton, which followed the banks of the River Hull from the North Bridge. Writing in 1903 historian Thomas Blashill noted: 'from the railway bridge at Wilmington may still be traced on the grass, after a light fall of snow, the High Road to Stoneferry'. Lime Street developed as part of the south end of the old track, as industries spread along the eastern banks of the river in the early 18th Century, including a sugar refiners', brick makers', rape-seed millers', soap boilers', ship builders' and lime burners', from whose kilns the street took its name, being first known as Lime-House Street in the 1790s.
Seen here in a 1930s Health Department photograph is the point at which Lime Street curves east towards Cleveland Street. On the right is the former Ship Launch Inn, established in the late 18th Century but closed in 1904. At the far end of the street was another pub, the Shoulder of Mutton, established in the 1850s and rebuilt by the Hull Brewery Co in 1896. The buildings on the right were cleared in the 1930s but the Shoulder of Mutton remained open until 1959.

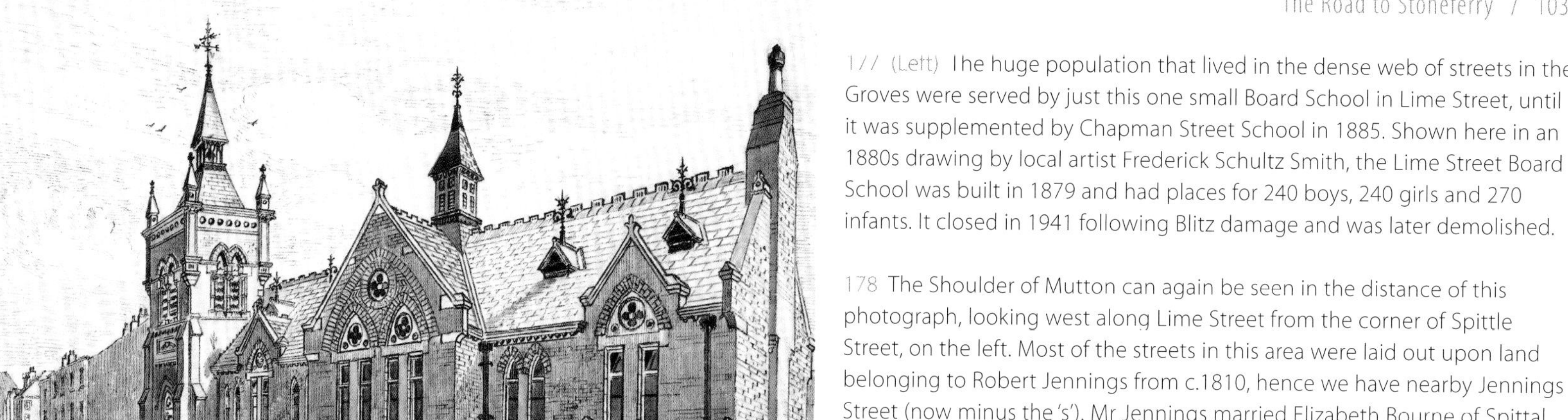

177 (Left) The huge population that lived in the dense web of streets in the Groves were served by just this one small Board School in Lime Street, until it was supplemented by Chapman Street School in 1885. Shown here in an 1880s drawing by local artist Frederick Schultz Smith, the Lime Street Board School was built in 1879 and had places for 240 boys, 240 girls and 270 infants. It closed in 1941 following Blitz damage and was later demolished.

178 The Shoulder of Mutton can again be seen in the distance of this photograph, looking west along Lime Street from the corner of Spittle Street, on the left. Most of the streets in this area were laid out upon land belonging to Robert Jennings from c.1810, hence we have nearby Jennings Street (now minus the 's'). Mr Jennings married Elizabeth Bourne of Spittal in Derbyshire, corrupted to Spittle Street, and Elizabeth re-married to a gentleman from Stockton in Cleveland, giving Cleveland Street its name. All of the housing in this area, and many of the streets, are now lost beneath industrial premises, most being demolished before the Second World War.

179 & 180 Plots of land and dwellings in Jennings Street, were for sale in the local press from c.1812. One notice stated that the street had good access to the 'new road to Wilmington and Stoneferry', but by 1814 only three inhabitants were listed in a trade directory of that year. The 1930s photograph on the right shows part of the south side of Jennings Street, nos.33 to 49, and the entrance to Thomas's Place in the centre of the picture. Below is another section on the south side, next to the junction with Lime Street, including nos.53 to 59 and the small entrance to Brown's Court. The street was heavily used following the opening of Scott Street bridge in 1902, but now serves simply as an access road to the remaining industries.

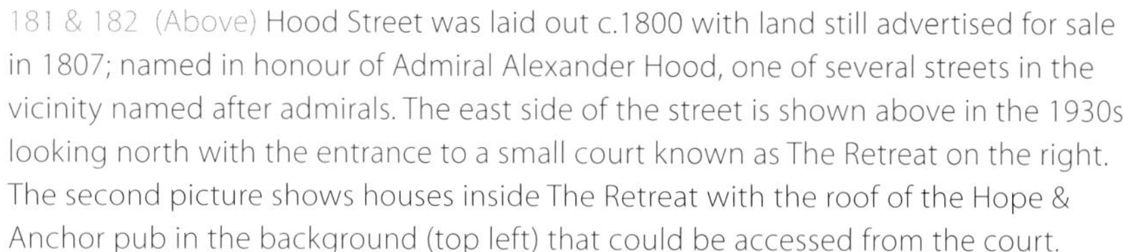

181 & 182 (Above) Hood Street was laid out c.1800 with land still advertised for sale in 1807; named in honour of Admiral Alexander Hood, one of several streets in the vicinity named after admirals. The east side of the street is shown above in the 1930s, looking north with the entrance to a small court known as The Retreat on the right. The second picture shows houses inside The Retreat with the roof of the Hope & Anchor pub in the background (top left) that could be accessed from the court.

183 The Hope & Anchor (seen here c.1926) was established in the late 1830s, initially being no.3 Cleveland Street, which at that time began at the junction with Jennings Street. The pub was re-built in 1938 and became a club during the 1970s. Since c.1980 this has been Spiders night club, incorporating the 1938 building.

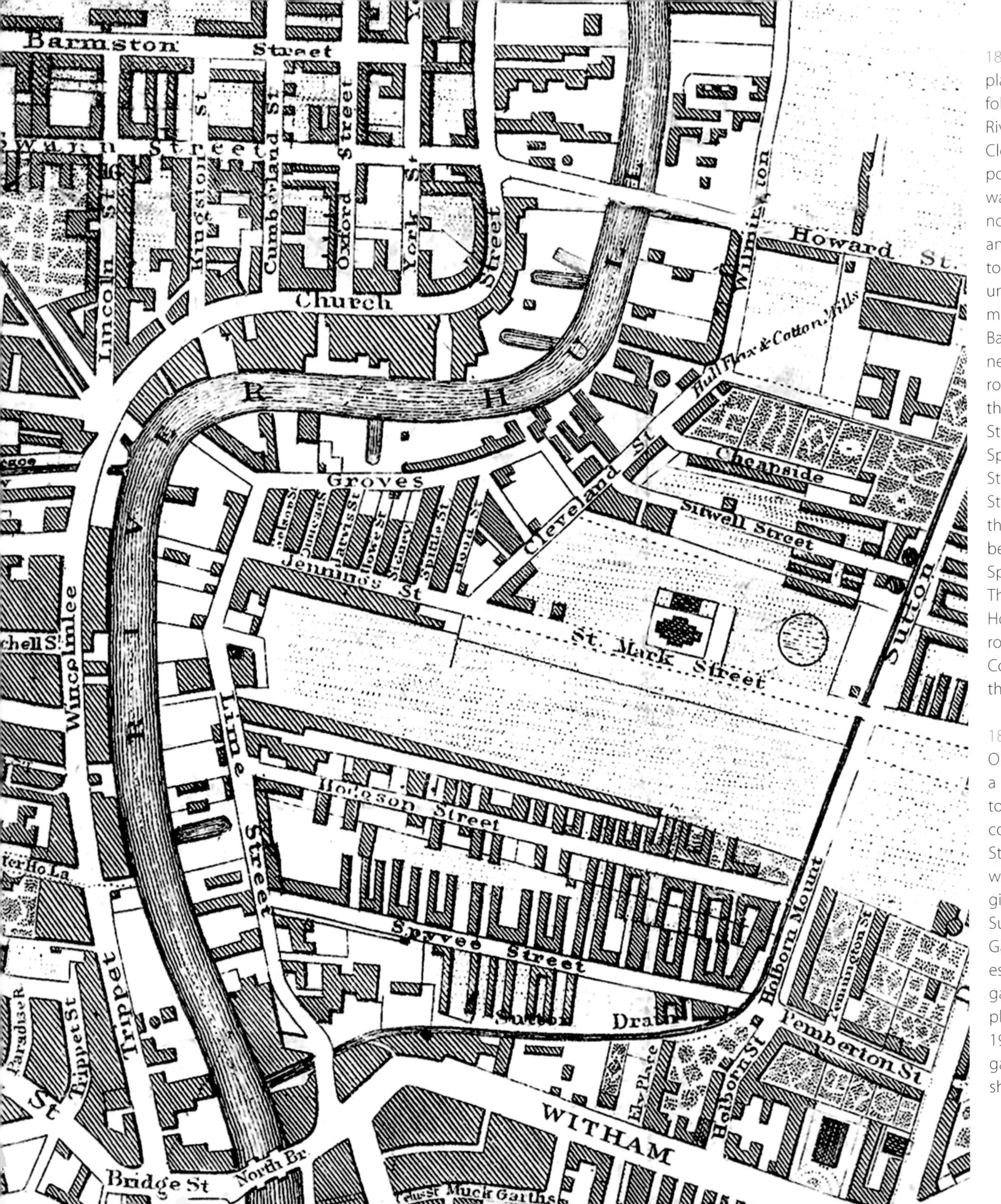

184 (This page) Peck's 1875 plan of Hull shows Lime Street following the route of the River Hull, into the Groves and Cleveland Street. From that point the route to Stoneferry was north via Wilmington – now part of Cleveland Street and Stoneferry Road. The route to Sutton was via Stoneferry unless you chose to follow the muddy track along the Sutton Bank, which was even harder to negotiate than the Wilmington route. Note that at this date the land south of Jennings Street remained open, and that Spyvee Street and Hodgson Street both ran east from Lime Street unbroken all the way to the Sutton Drain; Spyvee Street being laid out the ropery of Spyvee & Co (1780s to 1850s). The other long building above Hodgson Street, was also a ropery – that of Horncastle & Co, which remained in use until the 1870s.

185 (Next page) The 1908 Ordnance Survey plan shows a partially improved route to Stoneferry following the construction of New Cleveland Street from 1904. St Mark Street was also complete by then, giving better access to the Sutton, Southcoates, & Drypool Gas Cos works in Sitwell Street, established in 1847. The first gasometer shown on the 1875 plan was added to later in the 19th Century; the surviving gasometer, built in 1896, should be a Listed Building.

THE GROVES
Pearson Institute
Mission Hall
Crane
Scott Street Bridge
Seed Crushing Mills
Brewery
School
St. Mark's Church
Vicarage
ST. MARK STREET
JENNING STREET
MULGRAVE STREET
EGTON STREET
HODGSON STREET
SPYVEE STREET
WHITBY STREET
REDCAR STREET
CLEVELAND STREET
NEW CLEVELAND STREET
BENBOW STREET
DUNCAN STREET
JARVIS STREET
HOWE STREET
SIDNEY STREET
SIDNEY TER.
SPITTLE STREET
HOOD STREET
DURBAN STREET
HOLBORN STREET
Friends' B. Gd. (Disused)
Foredyke Stream
(Holderness Drainage)
Schools
DRY DOCK
Warehouses
High Water Mark of Ordinary Tides
Cato Mill
New Mill
North Bridge
TRAMWAY
WITHAM
Witham Saw Mill
School
Saw Mill
CŒLUS STREET
HYPERION STREET
MALTON STREET
BLENKIN STREET
TRIPPETT ST.
PARADISE ROW
MASON ST.
Burial Ground (Disused)
ALMA
GRAHAM'S ROW
EAST
Church
Urinal
Bank
P.O.
B.M. 11·1
B.M. 15·2
B.M. 15·3
B.M. 9·7
B.M. 11·9
B.M. 16·5
B.M. 18·6
B.M. 19·3
B.M. 20·4
B.M. 12·1
B.M. 12·4
B.M. 11·5
B.M. 9·6
B.M. 17·4
B.M. 19·1
B.M. 10·5
B.M. 14·3
ROMA TR.
ALMA TR.
EBOR TER.
GROVE TER.
ANSLEY TER.
KENT TER.
OXFORD TER.
YORK TER.
DURHAM TER.
SURREY TR.
LORNE TER.
JOSEPH'S TER.
SPYVEE TER.
MILLER'S TER.
SARAH ANN'S TER.
SOPHIA'S TER.
WILLIAM'S TER.
Travel. Cr.
Trav. Cr.
Tra. Cr.
F.P.
W.M.
P.H.
Chy.
Smy.

186 Seen here is the point at which the 'new' Cleveland Street met the old, recorded for posterity by local photographer Marcus Barnard c.1905. Jennings Street, where Cleveland Street originally began, is on the left and St Mark Street runs off the right (east) of the photograph. The ladies crossing the street may well have been heading home from work at Reckitt's in Dansom Lane, to their homes in the Groves and Sculcoates.

Seaton Brothers boot & shoe shop at no.2 Cleveland Street – the corner of St Mark Street, was established c.1883, and they had at least 10 shops in Hull by the 1920s, ceasing trading c.1930. It takes a vivid imagination to appreciate that this area, now even more dominated by trade and industry, once had its workforce living and shopping within walking distance. Another feature of this scene is the Cleveland Street Post Office, visible at the foot of the telegraph pole – below the painted wall advertising Raine's Groves Sheet Metal Works.

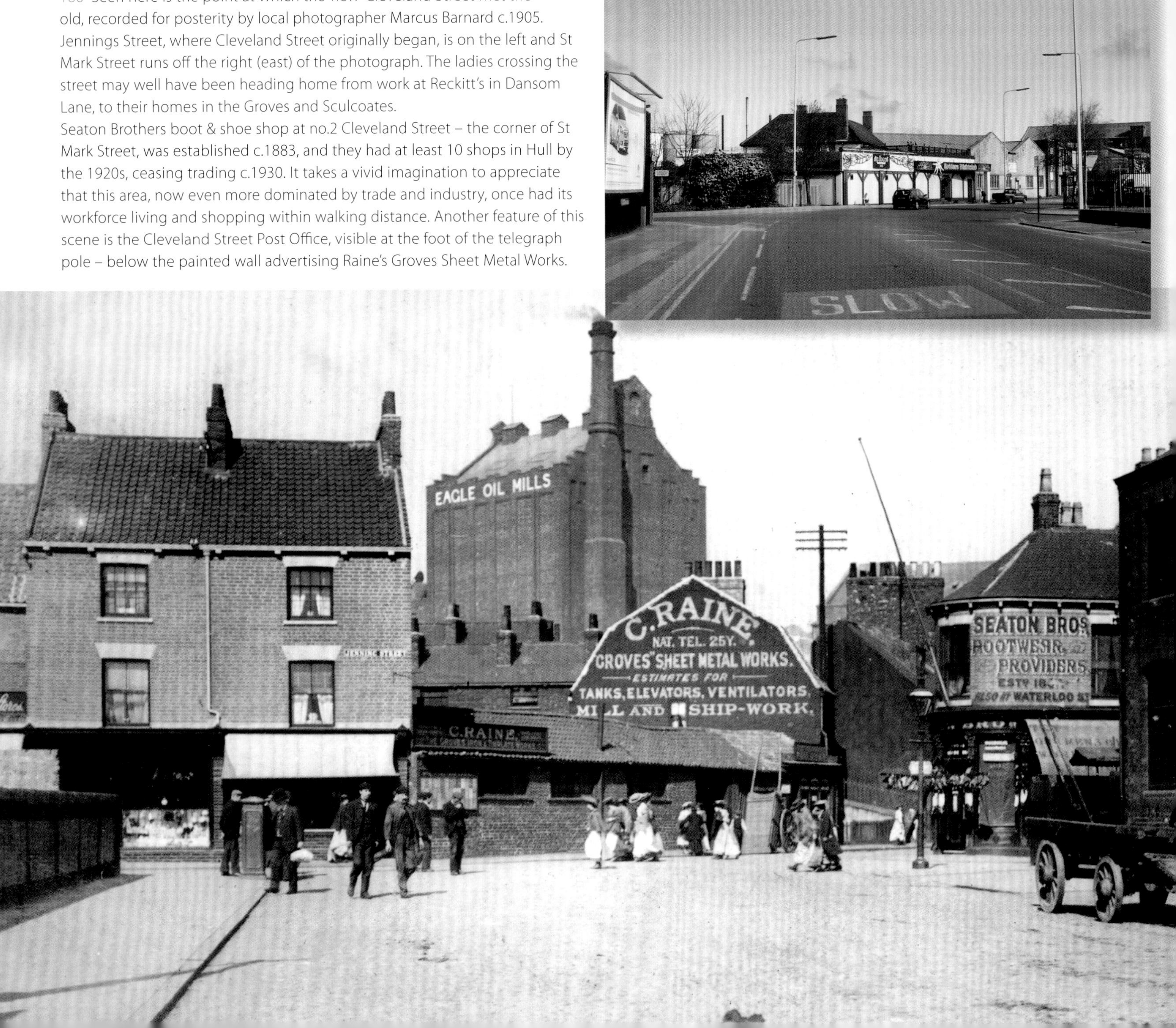

187 St Mark Street can be seen on the maps on pages 106-107, and was named after the church to which it led. The first stone of St Mark's Church was laid on Wednesday 9 June 1841, but due to a shortage of donations it was not completed until 1844. An article describing the laying of the foundation stone noted the street was 'newly laid out adjoining and in continuation of Jenning (sic) Street'. Designed by H F Lockwood, and built purposely to serve the rapidly growing population of the Groves, St Mark's had seats for 1,150 and cost £4,960 including the cost of the land. Half of the cost of the plot was donated by George Liddell who owned land on both sides of the Sutton Drain. Liddell charged tolls at a 'half penny hatch' for those wishing to cross the Sutton Drain at the end of the street, leading to Dansom Lane on the east side. Although named by 1848 it was not fully developed until the 1890s. Shown here in 1904 looking west, on the far right is St Mark's Vicarage, and behind the church and vicarage was St Mark's School; established in 1840, the school removed to the new building at the rear of the church in 1857, closing in 1940 following bomb damage.

The gasometers at the east end of the street were overshadowed by the distinctive spire of St Mark's, even though the top 25 feet had been lost during a storm in 1863. St Mark's was closed in 1948 following severe bomb damage in the Second World War. The site was demolished from October 1957, and has been the location for a variety of small businesses since, having been a timber yard for many years. Most of the housing in St Mark Street was cleared under a 1972 compulsory purchase order.

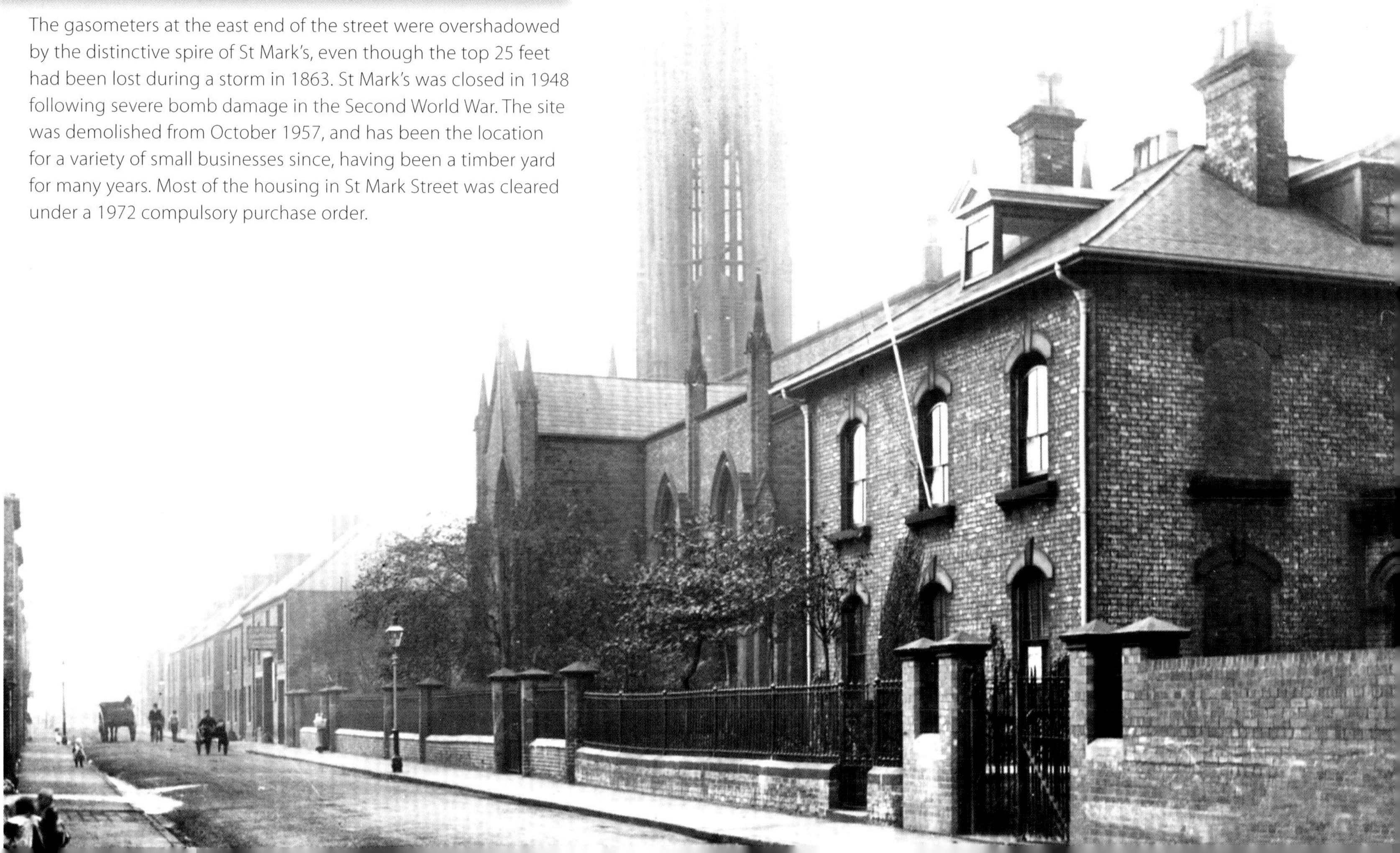

188 New Cleveland Street was cut through the property on the north side of Witham in the first years of the 20th Century. This formed a much wider connection with the junction of the original Cleveland Street further north, which remained just 30 feet wide. The narrow width of the old street posed a problem for a proposed tram service, as under the provisions of the Tramway Act of 1870 a minimum width of 35 feet was required to lay a line of double-tracks. Parts of the footpath were nibbled away here and there but the tram service never actually materialised (see page 115).

189 Some new streets were created along with New Cleveland Street. Mulgrave Street, Egton Street, Redcar Street and Whitby Street were laid-out in the early 1900s as one development with many terraces in between, such as Franklin Villas, shown here c.1910, which survives in part on the south side of Mulgrave Street.

The entrance to Spyvee Street from New Cleveland Street is shown here in a photograph of c.1905. No original property remains in Spyvee Street, most of the homes here having been demolished following more recent compulsory purchase orders in the 1960s and 1970s.

190 & 191 Hodgson Street was named after Edward Hodgson who was allotted land in this area under the Enclosure Awards of 1767. Much of the Georgian housing in the street was demolished from the late 1930s onwards in the so-called slum clearance schemes, although some remained until the 1970s.
The photograph on the top right shows typical original housing in the street, nos.85 and 87, with the entrance to Hodgson Court in between.
This arrangement of low quality court housing hidden behind slightly better quality buildings fronting the main street was common; the three small houses within Hodgson Court can be seen top left. The two houses and Hodgson Court were situated on the north side of the street (visible in the 1908 map on page 105), and were demolished before the Second World War, their site lost beneath offices and industrial premises that now cover the whole street. Only one original building remains in the street, the Ship Inn public house, established c.1814. This narrowly avoided being demolished when New Cleveland Street was created, and has had many alterations since, but continues to trade as it has for almost 200 years. Hodgson Street was the original location for Henry Blundell's paint and colour works, c.1807, later of Blundell's Corner and Bankside.

192 New Cleveland Street gave an opportunity for new shops in prime position along the extra frontage that was created. Quick to take up one of the new shops was of course the Co-op. Seen here is their branch no.16, which opened in 1905 and remained within the company until 1970. Situated at no.74 New Cleveland Street, on the corner of Egton Street, the grocery was later joined by a butchery branch next door at no.76 that closed in 1963. In 2010 several shops remain in this predominantly industrial area, serving the pockets of housing that have escaped the sweeping 20th Century clearance schemes. Until very recently the former Co-op was the long-standing premises of Blacklight International, who supplied sound and lighting equipment for entertainment venues and mobile discos. At the time of writing the shop was closed and for sale, as the modern photograph shows.

193 The north side of Chapman Street, where Chapman Street School can just be seen to the left, alongside nos.1 - 3 Chapman Street. No.3 was the shop of May Rawlinson at the time of this 1930s photograph, and on the right was Little Howard Street.

194 (Above) Cleveland Street looking north in the 1950s, before it was widened in 1962. In the centre, at the entrance to Cheapside, was the former Cotton Tree pub, named after the 19th Century cotton mills in this area. Visible on the right is the old refuse destructor, established in Chapman Street in the 1880s. Top left is today's much wider and busier road.

195 & 196 The origin of the name Wilmington has been lost over the centuries, but historically the line of Chapman Street marked the end of Cleveland Street and the beginning of Wilmington Lane.

During the late 18th Century and early 19th Century only the tenants of the land owner Henry Broadley could enter Wilmington, and others were barred from travelling further north across his land by a locked gate. During the 1850s a right of way was tested in the courts and the lane came into open use.

Wilmington was industrial from the early 19th Century and working class housing such as Cornwall Street, Withernsea Street and Bedford Street was built from the 1870s. Businesses such as Richard Sizer, established in 1866, sat alongside terraced housing built to home the workers. May Avenue, off Bedford Street, was typical, and is shown here c.1910, with Cornwall Street behind.

ESTABLISHED 1866

Richard Sizer Limited
Contractors to H.M. Government

Head Offices, Warehouses & Works.
Cornwall Street,
Wilmington, Hull.

Engineers and Allied Employers National Federation 1896

12th Sept 1937

Bought of Messrs Alexandra Steam Laundry

Richard Sizer, Ltd

Hydraulic & General Engineers,
Millwrights & Machinery Merchants.

Specialities
Cuber & Orbit
Worm Reduction Gears of all sizes
Gearing of all descriptions

Repairs done to all kinds of Machinery on the most reasonable terms.
Manufacturers of Hydraulic Presses, Pumps and Seed Crushing Plant.
Paint and Flour Mill Machinery.

ROLLS RE-GROUND AND FLUTED BY THE FINEST PLANT IN THE UNITED KINGDOM

197 (Right) Three sets of railway lines crossed the road through Wilmington, the earliest being the 1853 Victoria Dock branch line. This initially made use of a level-crossing that was replaced with this under-pass and rail bridge in 1911. The works were carried out to alleviate any delays to a proposed tram service to Stoneferry, and the process involved 100 men moving 90,000 cubic yards of earth, and laying 1,200 yards of brick and concrete sub-structure. Tram lines were laid under the bridge in May 1912, and the bridge was open to rail traffic by July. Sadly the tram service was never to reach Stoneferry and the tram lines laid here were never to be used.

198 The tram lines didn't even reach the next two bridges that crossed Wilmington Lane, by then known as part of the Stoneferry Road. This 1930s photograph shows a clear road surface under the two bridges constructed in the early 1880s to carry the Hull & Barnsley Railway Cos' lines to Alexandra Dock. Only the farthest of the three bridges shown here survives, near the end of Woodhall Street, and is still used by the goods line to King George and Queen Elizabeth docks. The other bridges were demolished during road-widening works in the 1980s, although a few courses of glazed white bricks remain in the still sunken roadway, as shown in the modern view.

199 & 200 Industry was attracted to Wilmington from the late 18th Century, by the transport link and water supply offered by the River Hull. A paper mill was here in the 1790s, glass works that are remembered in the street name Glass House Row, and 'Greenland Yards' for the whaling trade. Arguably the most well-known firm here was the cement works of G & T Earle established in 1809, contrary to the date on their shed.

Earle's works are shown above in a 1905 view made from the opposite side of the river, in Wincolmlee. The smaller picture on the right shows 'about ¾ of the workforce', according to the contemporary hand-written details on the back of the photograph, and dates from c.1900. Blue Circle Cement took over Earle's in 1967, transferring production elsewhere; the works were demolished in the early 1980s and the site is now partly used by Wyke Aggregates.

201 (Left) A ferry across the River Hull is recorded at Stoneferry from the 14th Century, replacing an even older stone ford that once stood further upstream. The last remnants of the ferry are shown here c.1900, where a ferry boat waits at the make-shift wooden platform that was used to board the boat. The Ferry House Inn, sometimes known as The Grapes, was established c.1820 and can be seen in this photograph on the north side of Ferry Lane. A new bridge over the river was planned from 1900 and in 1903 the Ferry Inn was demolished and replaced by a much larger building (see page 118).

202 Several churches were built in Stoneferry during the 19th Century. The first was the Bethel Wesleyan chapel, built c.1820, part of which was incorporated into Stoneferry Road School, both of which are now demolished. The Emmanuel Primitive Methodist chapel was built in 1871, just north of Maxwell and Street, and demolished in 1964.
St Saviour's Anglican church was built in 1903 to replace an older iron Mission hut. This was also demolished in 1981, but can just be seen, centre-left of picture 197 (page 115). The last surviving church was St John's Wesleyan, built in 1892 and shown here in 1906. This was demolished in February 1986, the site now occupied by Rievaulx Court (shown above).

203 (Above) This panoramic view is made possible by joining two photographs that were taken on 16th October 1905 to commemorate the opening of the first Stoneferry road bridge. They also record the final work taking place on the new Grapes Hotel on the far left, which still had open window frames and no clock fitted into its ornate tower. The site of the old ferry can also be seen on the far left. The bridge, and the widened Ferry Lane were integral parts of the 'Public Improvement' works carried out at locations around Hull from the 1880s. The first improvement in Stoneferry was the diverting and widening of the Stoneferry Road in 1886, which ran very close to the river just south of Ferry Lane, and was more than four feet below the river bank in places. A century later, in 1986 modern road improvements forced the demolition of the Grapes Hotel, and the bridge itself in 1989.

204 (Below) The ornate leaded windows of the Grapes Hotel Smoke Room were the backdrop of this c.1910 photograph, showing a 'road and country running' event. The two teams were the East Hull Harriers, with the monogram EHH on their shirts, and the Hull Harriers with a five-barred gate (formerly used by the Nightingales) on their shirts. Many running clubs were formed from c.1880, often created from athletic clubs. Increased leisure time in the late 19th Century gave working man his first taste of decent and regular recreation, and running, cycling and football clubs enjoyed a boom period. Running clubs such as these would often use improved public transport to travel to out of town events, such as this at Stoneferry. Events would more often than not end with singing and a pint in the local pub. The Ferry Inn, later the Grapes was for many years the headquarters of the Kingston Rowing Club, originally formed in 1861.

205 & 206 Further north along the River Hull was the Ship Inn, which had the potential to be considerably older than the Ferry House Inn. This was probably the location of the earlier stone ford across the river, which pre-dated the ferry, and was probably the reason that the inn was established here.

An early reference to the inn was at the Quarter Sessions in 1719, when Thomas Wheldale of Stoneferry was indicted for 'keeping a common alehouse without a licence at Stoneferry'. An old water-course called the Hantom Drain ran into the river behind the inn, adjacent to its garden (see page 120).

The larger photograph shows the original Ship c.1926, literally on the river bank, with its door facing the river and the Stoneferry waterworks on the west side. This old Ship was demolished c.1932 when the Hull Brewery Co built a new pub inland along Ann Watson Street (formerly Hospital Lane). The new pub is shown left in 1932, and remains relatively unchanged in 2010. Note the window sign in the old pub – Hull Brewery Double Stout – 9d for a large bottle.

207 & 208 These photographs show the centre of the hamlet of Stoneferry, and in the top image, the remains of the Antholme or 'Hantom' Drain can be seen. This was a 12th Century dike that ran south from Sutton to its outfall behind the Ship Inn. The medieval dike had mostly been superseded by an artificial ditch or 'leda' giving Leads Road its name. The handrail of the Hantom Bridge, which ran across the drain can also be seen leading to butcher Arthur Holmes' shop. In the centre are the three houses of Nancy's Terrace, and on the far left Elizabeth's Row. Also on the left is a pile of gravel, as the old drain was being covered over at this time, c.1905. In the second picture the drain is no longer visible and new curbstones surround a more defined Stoneferry Green.

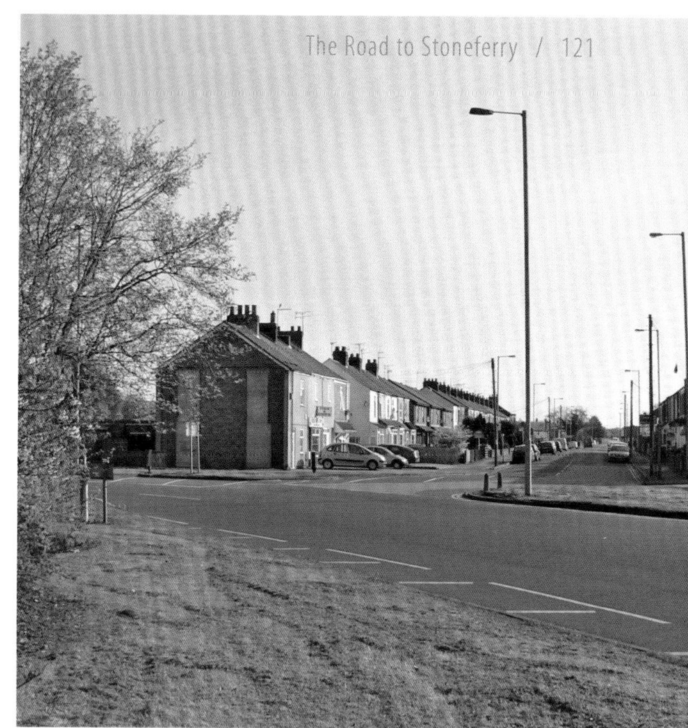

209 (Top left) A bandstand was erected on the newly created green in 1910, and is shown in this 1930s photograph that looks north-east into Leads Road. The bandstand remained until 1959 but the green, several houses and a pub (see page 122) were demolished in the early 1970s for the creation of the roundabout and new roads that gave access to the developing Sutton Fields industrial estate. In 1983 Stoneferry Road was widened again, resulting in the loss of more of Stoneferry's original buildings including shops and the old school.

210 (Right) Stoneferry was served briefly by the Sutton Victoria horse drawn bus service, seen here in Leads Road c.1905. Owned by Brian Lazenby, it ran from the Duke of York pub in Sutton to the White Horse pub in Carr Lane. Locals complained that of the 228 horse buses and waggonettes licensed in Hull one year, only four ran along Stoneferry Road. The reluctance of the operators to come to Stoneferry was probably due to the poor road surfaces and the low numbers that actually used the service. Though Stoneferry was taken within the extended Hull boundary in 1882, its transport links were slow to develop.

211 (Above) The New Inn first opened around 1872, and the original building can be seen on the far right of picture 212 (left). It was located at the end of Garbutt's Row, a terrace of houses on the north side of Leads Road, and was rebuilt as it appears above by Moors' & Robson's brewery in 1922.
The New Inn was lost for the development of the existing large roundabout in the 1970s.

212 As plans for Stoneferry's tram service floundered, a motor bus service was put into operation from mid-1909. This c.1910 photograph shows a typical vehicle in the fleet of six, parked outside the tiled frontage of the New Inn. Unfortunately the low usage and poor condition of the roads were as much an issue for motor-buses as they had been for the horse-buses, and the service ceased in April 1912. The motor-buses had barely lasted three years, and the residents of Stoneferry had another long wait before they received the first regular bus service in October 1921. Public transport to Stoneferry has run virtually uninterrupted ever since.

6 • Highgate, Lowgate & Marketgate

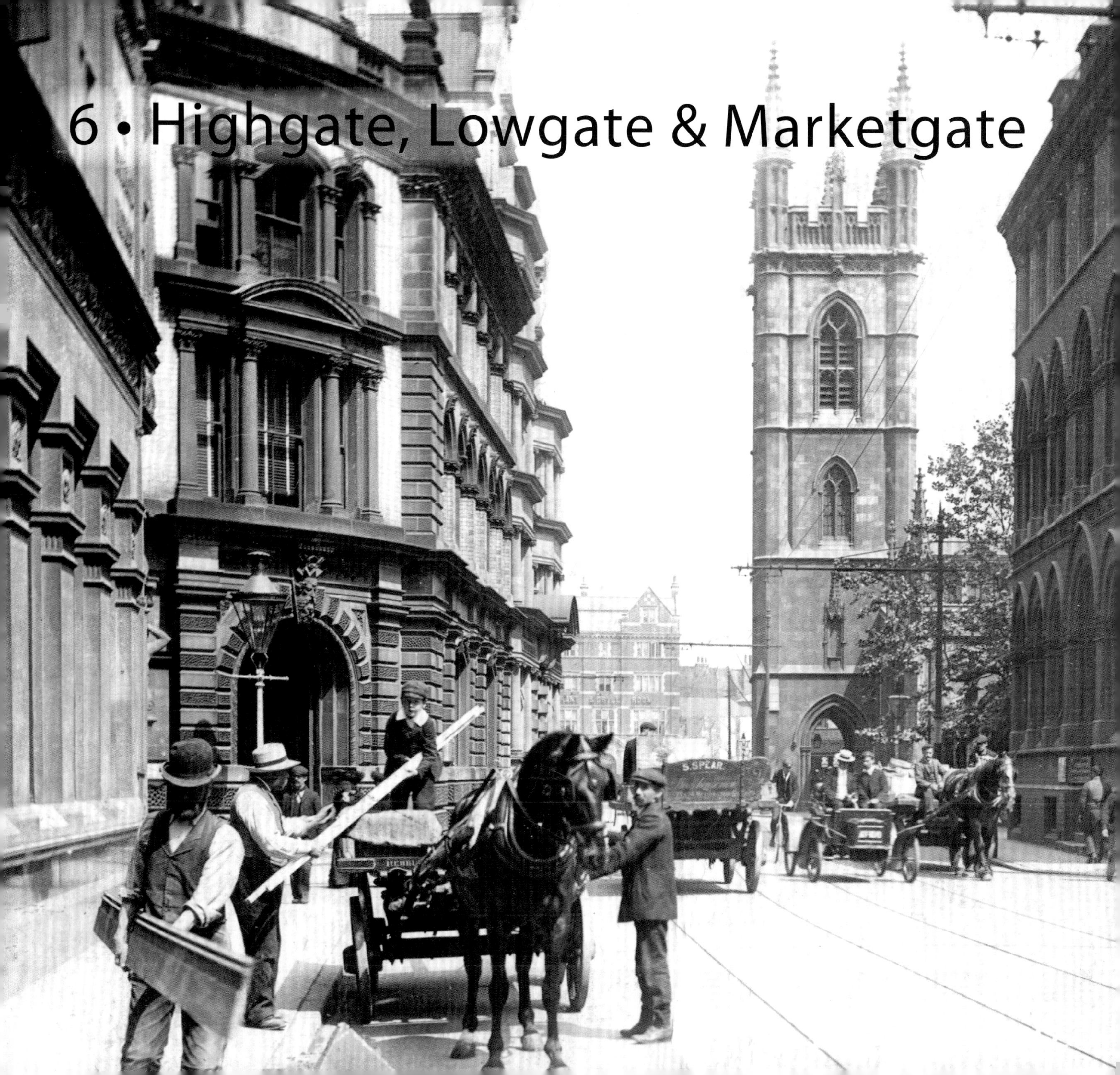

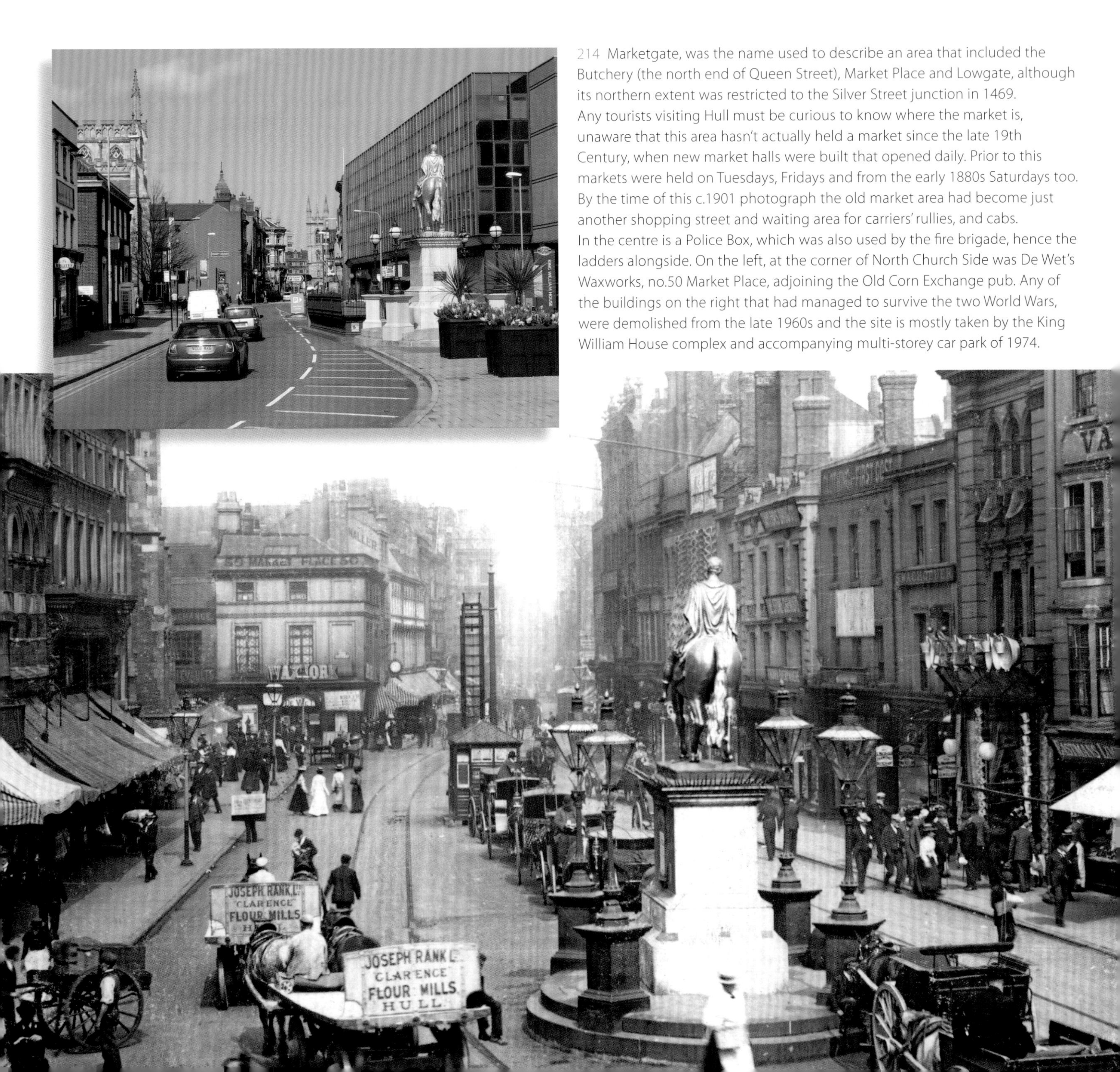

214 Marketgate, was the name used to describe an area that included the Butchery (the north end of Queen Street), Market Place and Lowgate, although its northern extent was restricted to the Silver Street junction in 1469. Any tourists visiting Hull must be curious to know where the market is, unaware that this area hasn't actually held a market since the late 19th Century, when new market halls were built that opened daily. Prior to this markets were held on Tuesdays, Fridays and from the early 1880s Saturdays too. By the time of this c.1901 photograph the old market area had become just another shopping street and waiting area for carriers' rullies, and cabs. In the centre is a Police Box, which was also used by the fire brigade, hence the ladders alongside. On the left, at the corner of North Church Side was De Wet's Waxworks, no.50 Market Place, adjoining the Old Corn Exchange pub. Any of the buildings on the right that had managed to survive the two World Wars, were demolished from the late 1960s and the site is mostly taken by the King William House complex and accompanying multi-storey car park of 1974.

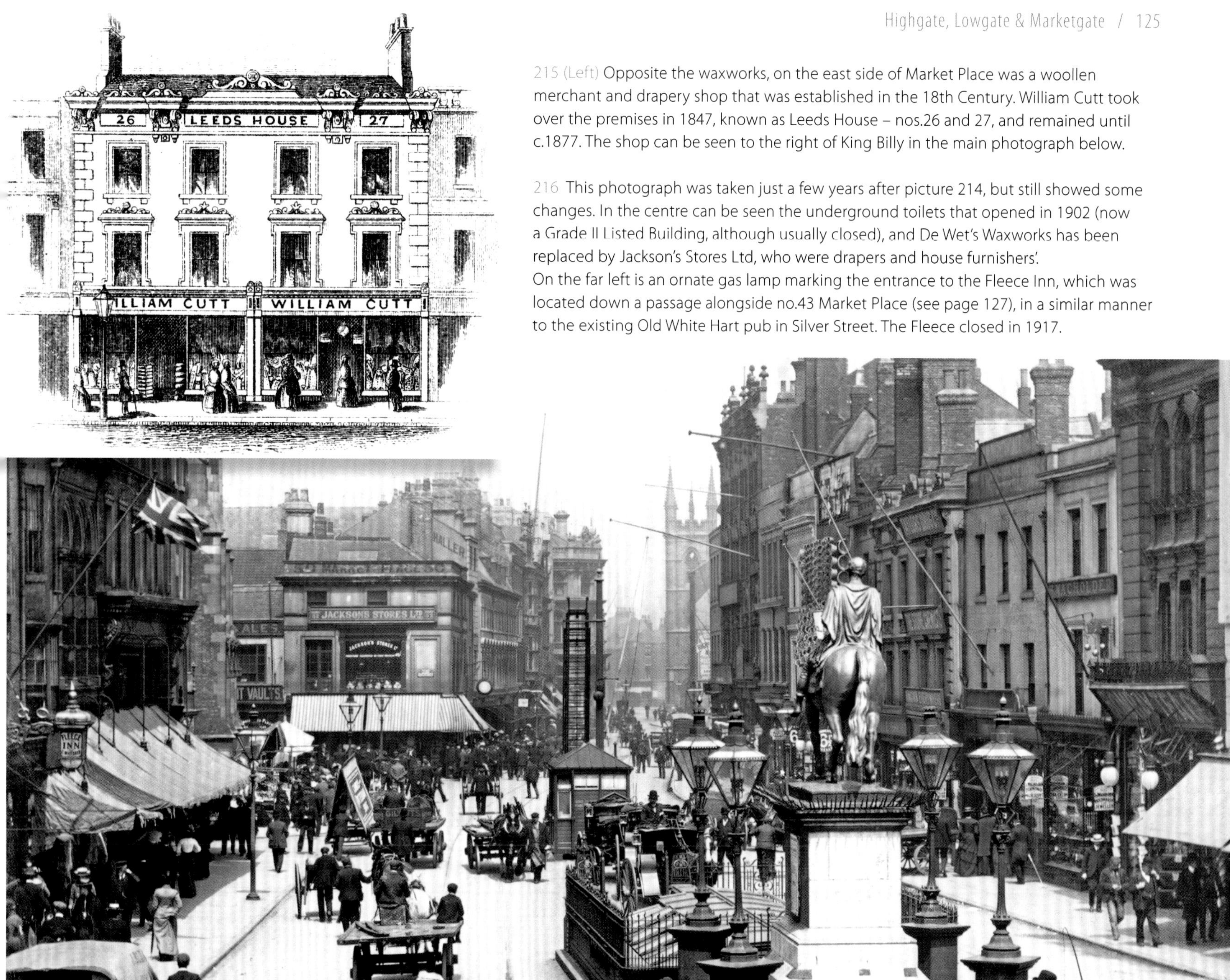

215 (Left) Opposite the waxworks, on the east side of Market Place was a woollen merchant and drapery shop that was established in the 18th Century. William Cutt took over the premises in 1847, known as Leeds House – nos.26 and 27, and remained until c.1877. The shop can be seen to the right of King Billy in the main photograph below.

216 This photograph was taken just a few years after picture 214, but still showed some changes. In the centre can be seen the underground toilets that opened in 1902 (now a Grade II Listed Building, although usually closed), and De Wet's Waxworks has been replaced by Jackson's Stores Ltd, who were drapers and house furnishers'.
On the far left is an ornate gas lamp marking the entrance to the Fleece Inn, which was located down a passage alongside no.43 Market Place (see page 127), in a similar manner to the existing Old White Hart pub in Silver Street. The Fleece closed in 1917.

217, 218 & 219 This drawing shows the southern aspect of Market Place, as it appeared c.1796. At this date it still resembled a typical market area and had not long since lost its elaborate Market Cross (1761). On the left is the original Cross Keys pub, and at the junction of Fetter Lane the Town Hall, incorporating much of the original Guildhall. In the centre The Butchery led to the original narrow Queen Street, with a new building on the opposite corner that replaced the old Jail and Guard House, demolished c.1792. On the far right was the entrance to Mytongate. As shown by the image below, this area retained its enclosed nature until Second World War bomb damage forced the demolition of many buildings here. The only surviving buildings at the south end are those that make up the King William pub, established as a Hellier's Coffee-House c.1833, and shown right in the 1960s. In recent years it has been extended to include the old Argenta Meat Company shop next door but one – that was once the premises of basket manufacturer J W Beeton (see next page).

220 (Left) It would be easy to assume the artist who drew the frontage of Beeton's shop and 'Perambulator Manufactory' at no.43 Market Place, had used artistic licence. The figures appear very small in comparison to the exaggerated size of the doors and windows. However, the photograph below showing Edwin Davis' shop next door at nos.45 to 48 Market Place, confirms the drawing was almost to scale. John William Beeton started out as a basket maker in Blanket Row in the 1840s, also trading from the Market Place shop from c.1866 until c.1873, maintaining just his basket manufactory in Blanket Row thereafter.

221 (Right) The story of Edwin Davis & Co is one of mixed fortunes. The business was established in Market Place around 1840, later expanding to take in shops on both sides. The re-fronted premises are shown here c.1910 complete with classical columns at either side of the huge shop frontage. In the Hull of the early 1900s, this was a prime spot but the shop was the victim of a bomb dropped from a First World War Zeppelin in 1915, and completely destroyed. Their replacement store, constructed in Bond Street c.1920, was also badly damaged during the Second World War. Davis's third store, built in Bond Street in 1952, remained open until the late 1970s, but is presently derelict awaiting demolition.

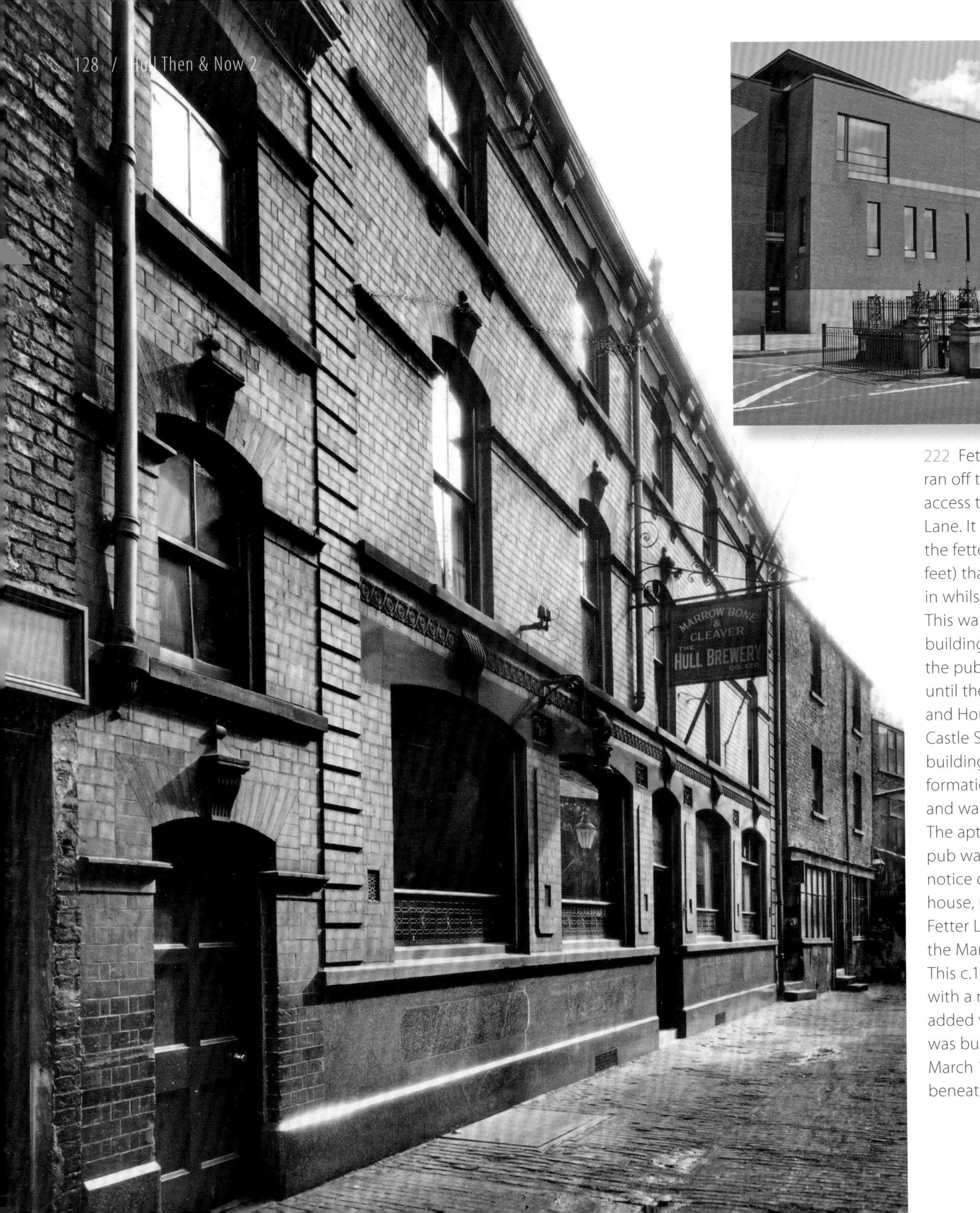

222 Fetter Lane was a narrow lane that ran off the east side of Market Place, with access to the High Street via Grimsby Lane. It most likely took its name from the fetters (a type of shackle for the feet) that prisoners may have been held in whilst at the 'House of Correction'. This was a dark, damp and cramped building that stood almost opposite the pub within Fetter Lane from c.1796 until the 1820s, when a combined Gaol and House of Correction was built in Castle Street. From that time the old building was used as a 'lock-up' until the formation of the police force in 1836, and was demolished in 1884.

The aptly named Marrowbone & Cleaver, pub was described in a newspaper notice of 1817 as: 'A new built dwelling house, used as a Public House, situate in Fetter Lane, and known by the name of the Marrow Bone and Cleaver'.

This c.1926 photograph shows the pub with a new frontage that was probably added when the 1887 Market Hall was built opposite. The pub closed in March 1957, and Fetter Lane is now lost beneath the Hull Magistrates Court.

223 (Below) The Malt Shovel pub was a sad loss when it was demolished in 1985, as at its core was a timber-framed dwelling dating from the 15th Century. The 1920s frontage was added by the Hull Brewery Co, but the original building can be seen in picture 224 (right) with a huge gas lamp at the door.

224 The Malt Shovel narrowly escaped demolition in 1902 when the new Market Hall was built in North Church Side. Complete with campanile tower, the modern design was the work of the first City Architect Joseph Henry Hirst and is shown here in its first months of opening. An almshouse adjoining the Malt Shovel, founded c.1700 and latterly known as Watson's Hospital, was demolished for the Market Hall.

225 (Left) Wholesale fruiterer Joseph Snaith, seen here c.1908, held stalls no.13 and 14 in the new market, which was initially intended for fruit and flowers only. Fruit had been sold in Market Place itself since the 16th Century, and from 1888 in a wholesale fruit and vegetable market in Corporation Field, Park Street until the 1960s. An extension to the covered market was opened in July 1950, but the 23 new stalls were restricted to selling butcher's meat.

226 (Right) White Horse Yard dated from the 16th Century, and took its name from the White Horse Inn that stood on the site; note the White Horse plaque on the first floor. Situated on the east side of Market Place, between Scale Lane and Church Lane its long narrow yard was home to many small businesses as recent as the 1920s, when it is shown here. By that time much of the back of the yard had been built upon, the frontage and entrance being demolished in 1937. The site, opposite Hepworth's Arcade, is now Aldgate House – a branch of The Bank of Scotland, and a small part of the rear yard is revealed once again – as a car parking area for the modern building.

227 Often confused as part of Lowgate, this section of road is still within Market Place, and until the late 15th Century market stalls stretched well beyond this point into what we now know as Lowgate. Each trade was allocated its own area within the Market Place, and this north end was the location of the fruit market until the 1750s. This c.1905 photograph looks north towards Lowgate, where the large banners of 'mantle makers' Goodson's Ltd, and Dale & Walker mark the junction with Silver Street on the left. Both sides of the road are lined with shops of every description; on the right a railway rully waits outside the former General Post Office, and sides of meat hang outside Witty & Easterby's butcher shop alongside the entrance to White Horse Yard. In 2010 very few shops survive on this stretch of road. A new Post Office is located on the opposite side of the street in the tobacconist' shop seen on the left – although confusingly, The Post Office have named it The Lowgate Post Office, no.63 *Market Place*.

228 Silver Street forms part of one of the very oldest alignments in the Old Town of Hull. Since the year 1320 this was part of Aldgate, which began at the Beverley Gate and included the alignments of Whitefriargate, Silver Street and Scale Lane. In the 14th and 15th Century Aldgate would have run through mainly open land and gardens at the west end near the gate, and housing would have been confined to this east end, near the river, the newly built St Mary's Church, and the merchants' premises and homes. Silver Street probably took its name from silversmiths', goldsmiths' and banks, located in the area from the 16th and 17th Centuries respectively.

We are fortunate that a house, probably built by Alderman William Foxley in the 1660s, survives off Silver Street. Known as the White Hart Inn since c.1778, its entry – White Hart Passage, gives us a clear picture of how enclosed the town's housing would have been at that time.

229 Lowgate was named as such, as it led to the Low-Market Gate, and one of the smaller entrances or 'posterns' through the 14th Century brick-built town walls. Beyond the small gate a wooden bridge led over the town ditch to the farmlands of Sculcoates north of the town.
Lowgate was widened during 1863-64, and its original width can be judged by the width of the road between the 1697 tower of St Mary's Church, and the buildings opposite; this section remains the narrowest point in the street. Throughout the late 19th Century improvements in the town, many large financial and mercantile buildings replaced lines of often ancient, shops and dwellings on both sides of the street. Thankfully many of these lofty buildings have remained, preserving the street's grand frontage, although few retain their original purpose and several are now used as pubs, bars or restaurants. The modern buildings add little in comparison.

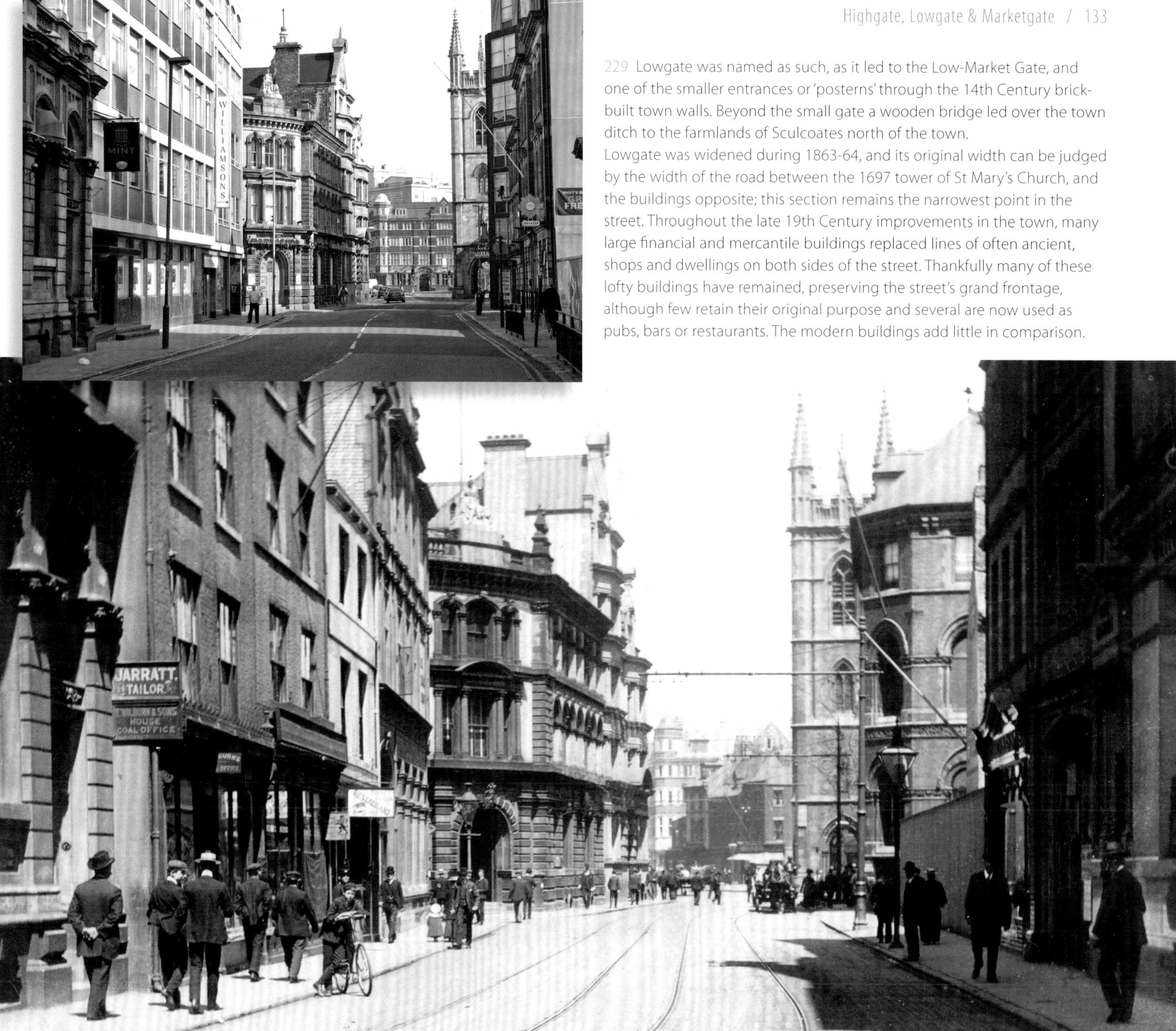

230 & 231 (Right) These are views of St Mary's Church that can no longer be made. On the left is the east end, revealed during the demolition of a printer's premises c.1907. Previously this was the site of Harrison's and Fox's hospitals, established c.1550, and Fox's in 1795; both were demolished c.1890. On the far right St Mary's is seen from the west side of Lowgate, on a site where the General Post Office was to be built in 1908 (now the Three John Scotts pub). In 1861-63 St Mary's was restored as we see it today, by George Gilbert Scott, a cousin of the vicar John Scott.

232 (Below) The Yorkshire Insurance Buildings were built adjacent to St Mary's yard in 1873, but demolished without protest in 1974 for the present rather mundane office block.

233 Chapel Lane is typical of the narrow streets that run from Lowgate to High Street, which when laid out had no need to be wider than the wheelbase of an old cart. The granite-setted road surface survives in some of the lanes, and after centuries of wear bears the tracks of iron-rimmed wooden wheels in many places. Most of the lanes took their names from the staithes, or jetties, that were used to load and unload goods from the Old Harbour into the merchants' riverside warehouses, mostly established before the west side of High Street was built upon. Seen here in 1905, with St Mary's casting a shadow across the street in the midday sun, Chapel Lane was home to several large businesses and the obligatory ale houses and breweries. J H Fenner was first established in Chapel Lane, and mineral water manufacturers James Hindle also had their works here. On the left of this 1904 photograph a printer's sign board can be seen; these buildings were built on the site of Harrison's and Fox's Hospitals in the late 19th Century and demolished c.1907 as seen in picture 230. The north side of Chapel Lane was lost in the late 1970s and early 1980s, and is now mostly occupied by the Combined Court Centre of 1988-90, which complements its surroundings well.

234 & 235 (Top and 2010 picture right) The creation of Alfred Gelder Street enabled the construction of some of Hull's finest Edwardian buildings. At the top of the page are exterior and interior views of Queen's Hall (of 1905), designed fittingly by architect Sir Alfred Gelder, as were the adjoining 'Waterloo Chambers' of 1905-06, which in part were offices for his business – Gelder & Kitchen. Surprisingly the whole block was demolished in 1965, the site remaining empty until the 1980s Combined Court was built here.

236 (Above left) The surroundings of the old Town Hall (1862-65 by Cuthbert Brodrick) were never felt appropriate, as it was flanked by slum housing, had the Kingston Gasworks behind it, and two old pubs and some of the most cramped court housing in the city across the road. The development of Alfred Gelder Street, which continued until 1910, provided a clean sweep in which most of the troublesome buildings were removed. This 1902 photograph shows the old Town Hall, with new buildings in progress directly opposite.

237 Until Alfred Gelder Street was cut through from 1901, Lowgate ran north, uninterrupted, as far as what is now known as Guildhall Road. This modern alignment roughly marks the site of the old town walls. This section of the 1889 Ordnance Survey plan illustrates the congestion and poorly laid out nature of the old town. The overcrowded courts and alleys were the ideal setting for crimes of every description, and a breeding place for disease. In just the small area shown here there were also at least 12 pubs, whereas in 2010 there are just two.

The old Town Hall and adjoining buildings were inadequate to meet the demands of Hull's huge economic growth, and subsequent population increase during the late 19th Century. The old Town Hall was demolished from 1911, and the present Guildhall opened in 1916.

When St Mary's Church was built c.1330, it faced the site of a dilapidated set of buildings dating to 1297. This had been the home of Edward the First's 'keeper of Hull', but had been badly maintained during the early 14th Century.

The building passed to the Pole family around 1330, who rebuilt it as a large manor house known as Suffolk Palace, and enlarged it in 1380 when it became known as Court hall. The De La Poles were lords of the Manor of Myton at that time.

The house and its grounds were demolished and broken up from the 1660s, but pieces did remain, such as an octagonal room and small adjoining building that was adapted as a Baptist Chapel in 1736. This survived until 1936, and its location can be seen on the plan as 'Lincoln's Inn Buildings'. Streets in the area, such as Manor Street and Bowlalley Lane, mark the site of the palace. Despite being a busy thoroughfare, this historic area retains some of Hull's finest architecture.

238 One of the blocks demolished for the construction of Alfred Gelder Street was this, which stood immediately south of the old Town Hall, the railings of which can be seen at the bottom right of the picture. St Mary's church can be seen on the extreme left, and in the centre the entrance to one of Hull's lost streets – Leadenhall Square. At the time of this late 1890s photograph the Georgian shop front, no.66 Lowgate, was a tobacconist' and parcel receiving office for the L & NWR. Upstairs were the offices of fish curers' Fountain & Co, and in Leadenhall Square, the offices of the Hull Corporation Sanitary Dept.

239 (Top left) The stylish Royal Exchange Buildings, built c.1905, can be seen on the left of this pre-First World War photograph looking south along Lowgate. These were amongst the first buildings demolished in this block from the late 1960s onwards, and this is now the site of the Combined Court Centre. On the right is the General Post Office, built in the Edwardian Imperial style in 1908-09 to the designs of W Potts, and officially opened 24 July 1909.

240, 241 & 242 The General Post Office is seen here in views dating from c.1909, including the 'instrument room', a public counter, and the many postal staff in the rear courtyard. The buildings suffered heavy damage in the Second World War, but repairs carried out in 1950 matched the original stonework seamlessly. In 2000-01 the redundant buildings were converted to other uses including snooker rooms, a restaurant, private apartments and a public house known as the Three John Scotts, all of which remain open in 2010.

243 (Left) High Street, known variously through history as Highgate, Hull Street or King Street, is almost certainly the oldest alignment in Hull. As Hull was first established in the late 12th Century, the very first buildings that existed were built alongside the long winding lane that followed the course of the river Hull. This c.1933 photograph shows the southern extent of High Street, where it joins with Humber Street, with the premises of Hall's Barton Ropery on the right. Known as Etherington House, the building dated from c.1673, but was re-fronted about 1870 and demolished in 1947. Just to the north can be seen the entrance to Rottenherring Staith, the alignment of which, is still visible today but has no original buildings.

244 (Right) The open foreground on the right of picture 243 had been the site of this small alehouse, the Dog & Duck, once part of a longer building that dated from the 1600s. The rest of the building was demolished in 1864 to make way for the construction of the South Bridge, completed in 1865. The Dog & Duck had been a pub since c.1800 but was demolished shortly after closure in 1908.

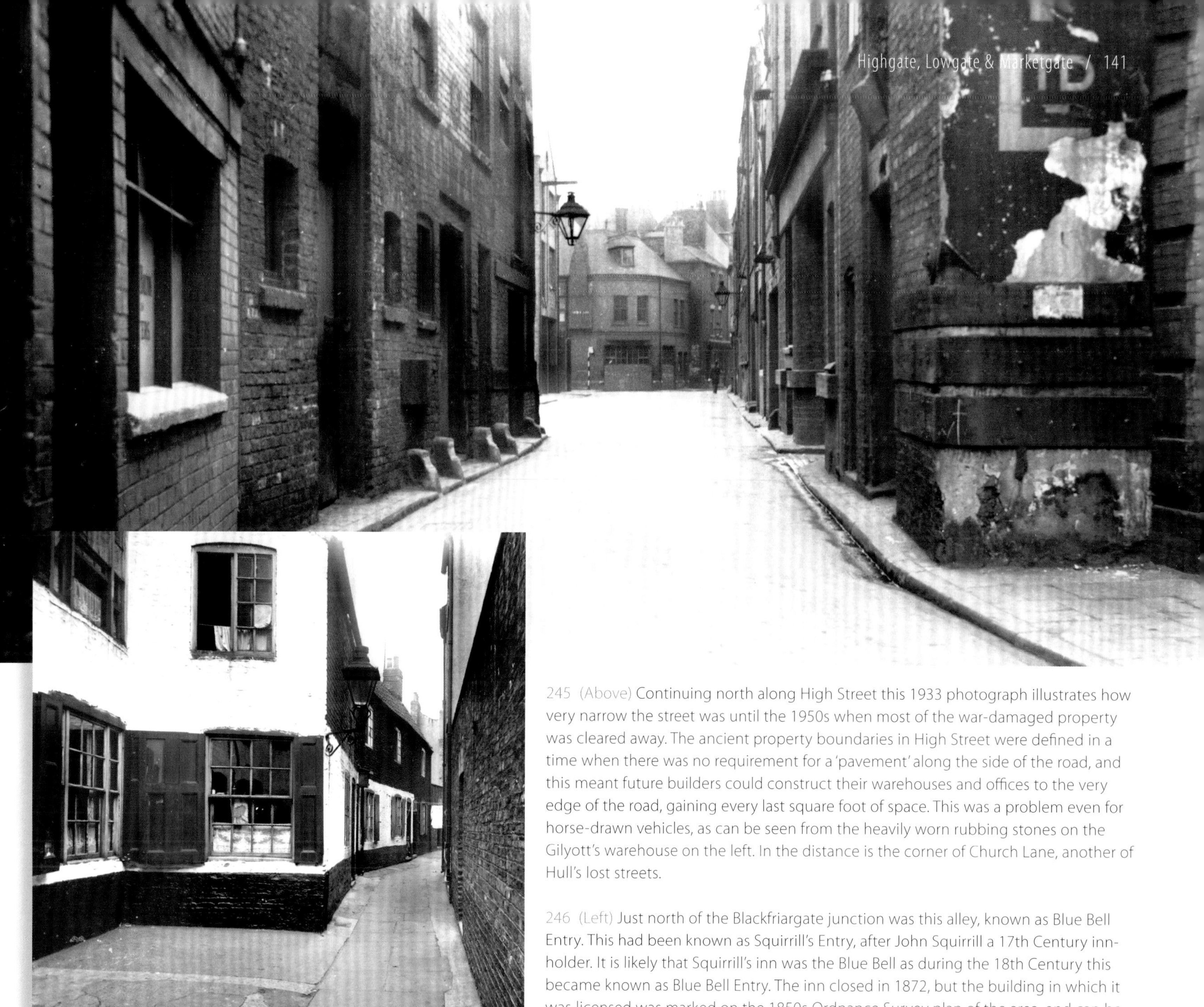

245 (Above) Continuing north along High Street this 1933 photograph illustrates how very narrow the street was until the 1950s when most of the war-damaged property was cleared away. The ancient property boundaries in High Street were defined in a time when there was no requirement for a 'pavement' along the side of the road, and this meant future builders could construct their warehouses and offices to the very edge of the road, gaining every last square foot of space. This was a problem even for horse-drawn vehicles, as can be seen from the heavily worn rubbing stones on the Gilyott's warehouse on the left. In the distance is the corner of Church Lane, another of Hull's lost streets.

246 (Left) Just north of the Blackfriargate junction was this alley, known as Blue Bell Entry. This had been known as Squirrill's Entry, after John Squirrill a 17th Century inn-holder. It is likely that Squirrill's inn was the Blue Bell as during the 18th Century this became known as Blue Bell Entry. The inn closed in 1872, but the building in which it was licensed was marked on the 1850s Ordnance Survey plan of the area, and can be seen on the left of this 1920s photograph. The Health Department photographer who took the photograph was looking west, and it is no surprise that he was recording the 30 dwelling houses that shared this small space, prior to demolition c.1931.

247 & 248 Temple's Entry, a small court just south of Scale Lane, was entered through the medieval, timber-framed building on the left. Its architectural features, including a jettied first floor, would now be a highlight of Hull's Museum Quarter, if this section of High Street had not been demolished from 1905, leaving the gap shown in picture 249 (next page and below). The large image here is from 1904, and the image above shows the revealed interior of the court, in a c.1906 photograph.

249 Looking north towards the Scale Lane junction, this 1933 photograph shows locals in the gap left by the demolition of Temple's Entry and adjacent property. All of the buildings south of Scale Lane have now gone, and the site of this image is now mostly occupied by a 1990s office building.

250 & 251 Th[illegible] Kings Court c.1924. On the left are the remains of some of the ten or so homes t[illegible] faced each other in this tiny space, and on the right is the entrance from High Street. This site is now occupied by the car park of [illegible] Argos store.

252 (Right) Another 1933 view of High Street, approaching the corner of Chapel Lane, where an old pub is for sale. In the distance more old jettied buildings project out into the street.

253 (Below) The Edinburgh Packet, no.163 High Street, had been a pub since at least 1732, taking its later name from a regular packet-ship to Scotland. The pub closed in 1929 and was demolished soon after. The site is now used by Flavours Cafe, built on the site of the Epicure Cafe, at no.165, also visible in this 1926 photograph.

254 & 255 The Wilberforce Inn, and the adjoining premises, are the timber-framed and jettied buildings visible in the distance of picture 252 (previous page). Towered over by the Globe Warehouse on the opposite side of the street, and adjoining the large premises of paper merchants Ash & King, and ships chandlers John Good & Sons to the north, these buildings are recorded in documents from the early 17th Century, but were probably a great deal older. 'Wilberforce Inn' was a new name (c.1904) for an inn known as the Yarmouth Arms since the 1730s. The Wilberforce Inn closed in 1908, just as the photograph on the right was taken. In the centre of the jettied buildings is the entrance to George Yard, named after the ancient George & Dragon Inn, (see below). At the other side of the entrance, marked by the second flag-pole, was a slightly younger pub, known as the George Yard Inn. This faced High Street (no.170) and traded from c.1618 until 1910. Within George Yard was the George & Dragon Inn, one of Hull's oldest alehouses, whose origins can be traced by name to the 1670s. It is likely that it existed much earlier however, and was probably that part of a 'brewhouse' that was recorded on this site in 1455.

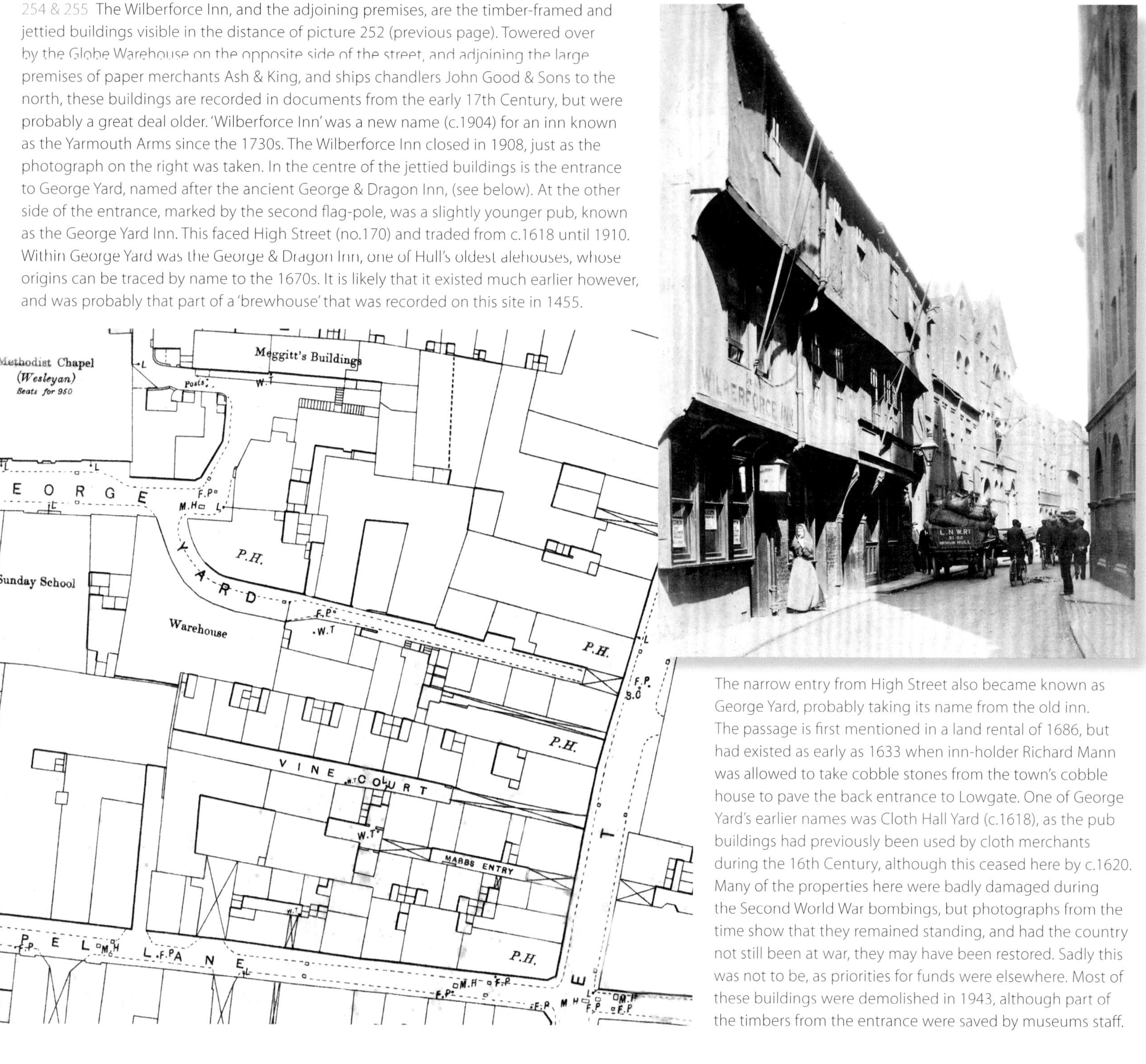

The narrow entry from High Street also became known as George Yard, probably taking its name from the old inn. The passage is first mentioned in a land rental of 1686, but had existed as early as 1633 when inn-holder Richard Mann was allowed to take cobble stones from the town's cobble house to pave the back entrance to Lowgate. One of George Yard's earlier names was Cloth Hall Yard (c.1618), as the pub buildings had previously been used by cloth merchants during the 16th Century, although this ceased here by c.1620. Many of the properties here were badly damaged during the Second World War bombings, but photographs from the time show that they remained standing, and had the country not still been at war, they may have been restored. Sadly this was not to be, as priorities for funds were elsewhere. Most of these buildings were demolished in 1943, although part of the timbers from the entrance were saved by museums staff.

256 (Left) Very little survives from this 1933 view, looking north towards the Wilberforce House entrance. Built in 1660, the wall of Wilberforce House can just be seen on the right, and is one of only two surviving buildings in this view – the other being Oriel Chambers, whose first floor 'oriel' window can be seen with a 'To Let' sign centre right. Everything else here was demolished during and after the war.

257 (Below) The entrance to George Yard can be seen on the right of picture 256, and this was the view further into the yard as it opened out towards the Lowgate end.
Demolition was underway for the construction of Alfred Gelder Street in this 1905 photograph, sealing the fate of the George Yard Chapel of 1785, which was demolished during the works.

258, 298 & 260 In a post-war redevelopment plan for Hull by Patrick Abercrombie and Sir Edward Lutyens, Wilberforce House was to be the only building left in High Street. The illustration above shows how close we came to High Street being cleared for a new road network. The c.1910 image on the left shows yet more medieval timber-framed buildings opposite Wilberforce House, including the former Globe Inn on the far right. Many of the courts and alleys behind this frontage were demolished for Alfred Gelder Street but as the c.1947 photograph below shows, many remained after the war. Most of the long terrace adjoining Wilberforce House was demolished in the late 1940s, but nos.23-24, built as a pair c.1760, were saved. Restored in 1957, they re-opened as the 'Georgian Houses', partly visible far right.

261 (above) A 1940s photograph looking into High Street from Alfred Gelder Street, with John Scott's Ceres warehouse on the left. In 1981 developer Ben Hooson began to convert the warehouse into flats, but a serious fire meant the building had to be demolished. Undeterred Ben rebuilt the warehouse as we see it today.

262 High Street continues north beyond Alfred Gelder Street, and this early 1960s photograph shows buildings in this section, near the entrance to Salthouse Lane, which remained until the 1970s. 1980s apartments now occupy this site.

263 & 266 On the far left of picture 262 (previous page) is the corner of Salthouse Lane. Salthouse Lane Staith on the opposite side of High Street, was lost when the original Drypool Bridge was built in 1888, and much more property was lost when Alfred Gelder Street was constructed from 1901. Some of the buildings lost from the north side of Salthouse Lane are shown in these photographs. On the left is a 1930s view showing the entrance to Scurfield Square, at the Lowgate (west) end, and above a c.1974 view made shortly before demolition showing the east end, with the rear of Charles Ware's premises, which fronted High Street. Much of the street had already been demolished in the late 1960s and just two original buildings now survive.

265 High Street ends at what used to be called North Walls, the location of the North Gate within the town walls; beyond this is Dock Office Row. This corner is shown above in an engraving of Johnson's 'National Paint Works', with High Street running across the bottom. Johnson's works were constructed in 1890, their arched entrance built on the former entry to Fleece Inn Yard, and their site partly occupying the site of a former brewery, and many small dwellings within the old courtyard.

266 No.197 High Street, near the north end, had been the site of an alehouse since at least 1736. First known as The Fleece, or Golden Fleece, it was renamed the Highland Laddie c.1904, which it remained until closure on 7th December 1961. At the rear of the pub was a brewery, which dated from c.1792, and was accessed via Fleece Inn Yard adjoining the pub. The pub and the former entry are shown here in 1926. Much of this north-east end of High Street is now occupied by apartments built mostly during the 1980s.

7 • Myton

268 (Right) The chapter title page image shows partially demolished property on the east side of Fawcitt Street during the 1930s. The tallest building still had a wall-bracket where an inn sign once hung. This was the Grapes Tavern, established c.1810 by Robert Snell, a sawyer by trade. The Grapes held a full alehouse licence, but was closed c.1910 when £1,600 was paid in compensation. Fawcitt Street, laid out from c.1803, was probably named after mason John Fawcitt, and ran off the north side of Great Passage Street. Its north end was later blocked by council schools, built on former garden land on the south side of Osborne Street. This c.1912 view shows the street looking north; note the Georgian door cases, which had been removed in the previous image. Fawcitt Street was demolished in the 1960s and the site is now lost beneath the Staples office supplies store.

269 (Left) Photographs of this part of Hull, generally known as South Myton, are scarce to say the least, and it is fortunate that in cases where photographs may not exist we have drawings made by the artist F S Smith. This view was made by Smith in the 1890s, and shows Great Passage Street looking west from the corner of Lower Union Street on the immediate right. On the left is a beer-house that was established here c.1803, and latterly known as the Lord Napier. This was demolished during the Great Passage Street improvement and widening scheme of 1898-99 when the south side of the street was cleared of all buildings. Most of the property shown in this view is now lost beneath the road intersection where Ferensway meets the A63 – Castle Street.

270 (left) Lower Union Street was the next street to the west of Fawcitt Street, and was made up of the same mixture of mostly poor quality buildings. This was another of the streets laid out from c.1800 in South Myton, as Hull grew beyond the confines of the Old Town. Both Upper Union Street and Lower Union Street were probably named in reference to the union of Great Britain and Ireland, formed in 1801. The two other streets on this north side – Burton Street and Fawcitt Street, were culs-de-sac. Seen here in the 1930s are nos.48 & 50 Lower Union Street, on the west side near the corner of Great Passage Street, to the left of this picture. The demolition of Lower Union Street began in the late 1950s when Ferensway was extended south beyond the Anlaby Road.

271 (Right) Joseph's Place was typical of the courts that were tucked away behind the frontage of almost every main street in South Myton. The ramshackle housing was accessed via a narrow passage on the west side of Lower Union Street, next to the Gate public house. This 1931 photograph shows some of the 14 blind-back houses that were situated in the court, which had two sections in an L-shaped arrangement. This photograph shows the second, even darker section, entered via another alley leading from the first. The 1881 Census recorded 46 residents in the 11 inhabited houses of Joseph's Place, with two of the houses having seven residents in each.

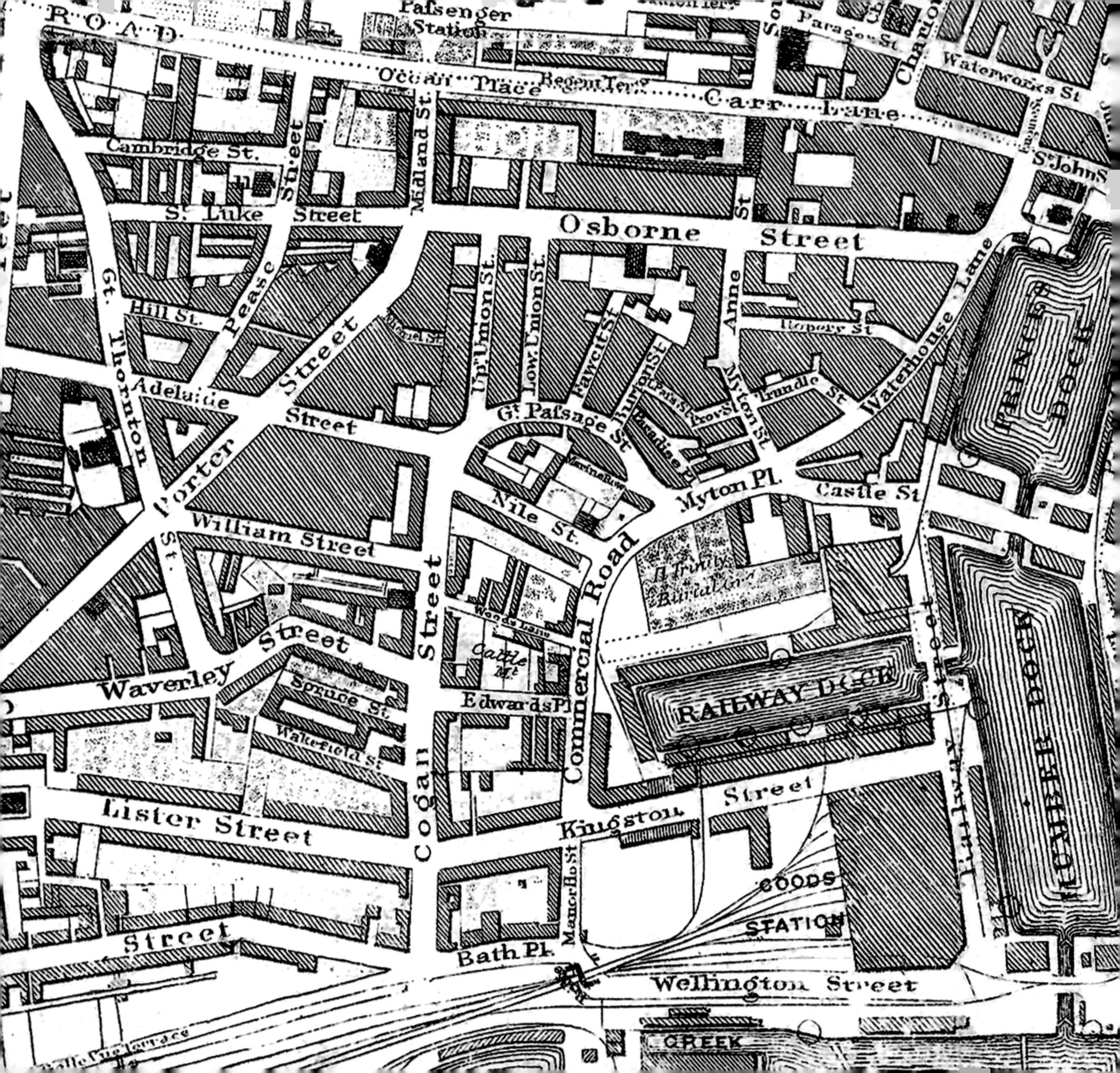

ROAD
Passenger Station
Paragon St
Charlot
Ocean Place
Regent Terr
Carr Lane
Waterworks St
Cambridge St.
Street
Midland St
St Johns
St. Luke Street
Osborne Street
Gt Thornton
Pease Street
Hill St.
Up. Union St.
Low. Union St.
Anne
Ropery St
Waterhouse Lane
PRINCES DOCK
Faycitt St.
Mytonn St
Trundle St
Adelaide
Street
Gt. Passage St
Myton Pl.
Castle St
Porter St
William Street
Nile St.
Commercial Road
H. Trinity Burial Gd.
Street
Woods Lane
Cattle Mt
RAILWAY DOCK
Waverley
Street
Spruce St
Edwards Pl
Wakefield St
Cogan Street
Street
HUMBER DOCK
Lister Street
Kingston
Railway
GOODS
STATION
Street
Manor Host
Bath Pl.
Wellington Street
CREEK

272 (Previous page) This section of Peck's 1875 plan of Hull shows most of the streets in South Myton discussed in this chapter. It is interesting to note that even in the 1870s some open garden areas still remained undeveloped, but not for long, as housing demand grew.
The whole area is now divided by the Castle Street development of the early 1970s, although demolition began in this area with compulsory purchase orders issued in 1966-67.
The granite-setted surface of Upper Union Street remains, now the location of 1950s housing and a 1980s apartments known as Amy Johnson Court (below).

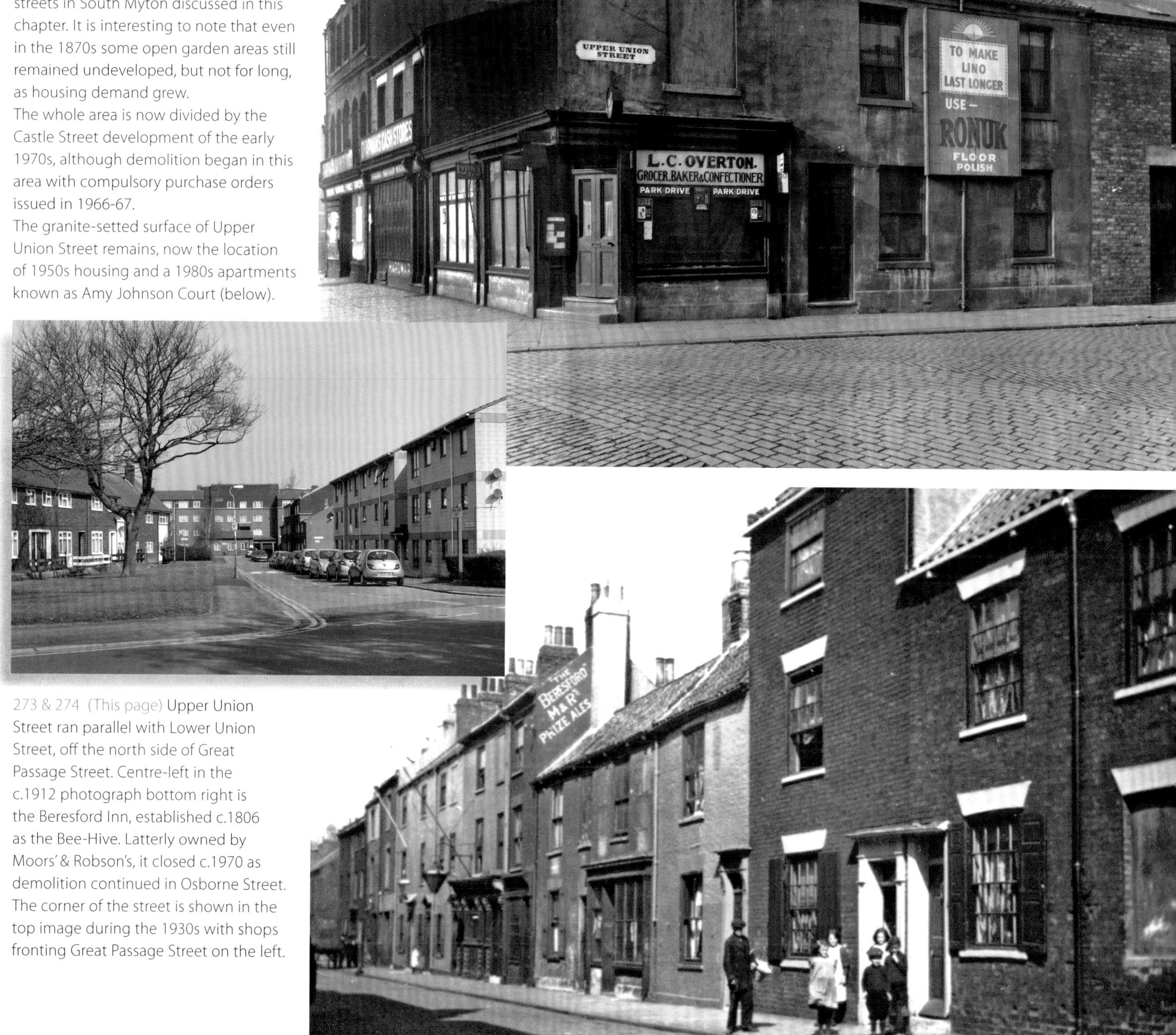

273 & 274 (This page) Upper Union Street ran parallel with Lower Union Street, off the north side of Great Passage Street. Centre-left in the c.1912 photograph bottom right is the Beresford Inn, established c.1806 as the Bee-Hive. Latterly owned by Moors' & Robson's, it closed c.1970 as demolition continued in Osborne Street. The corner of the street is shown in the top image during the 1930s with shops fronting Great Passage Street on the left.

The three blocks were demolished in 1970 and the site of the Artisans' Dwellings is now a garden area in the shadow of the 1980s William Booth House.

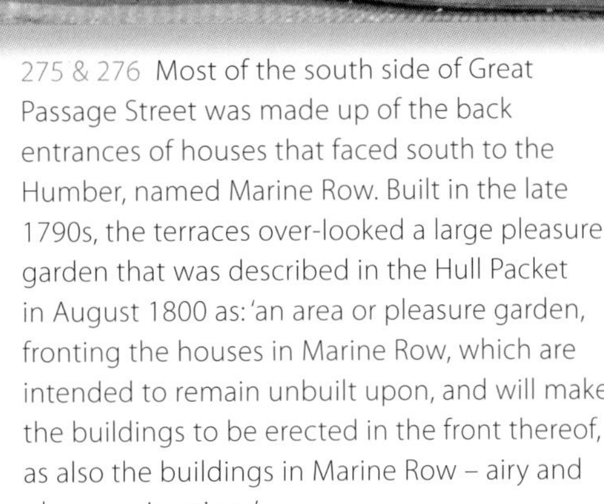

275 & 276 Most of the south side of Great Passage Street was made up of the back entrances of houses that faced south to the Humber, named Marine Row. Built in the late 1790s, the terraces over-looked a large pleasure garden that was described in the Hull Packet in August 1800 as: 'an area or pleasure garden, fronting the houses in Marine Row, which are intended to remain unbuilt upon, and will make the buildings to be erected in the front thereof, as also the buildings in Marine Row – airy and pleasant situations'.

The south side of the street was demolished when Great Passage Street was widened in 1899, and re-built with several large buildings. Three blocks of dwellings, created as Hull's first council housing – and first flats, were the first to be erected in 1900. Designed by the City Architect Joseph H Hirst, these were amongst many housing schemes built to re-home residents displaced by the 'improvement works' in the city centre. Named Marvel Dwellings, De La Pole Dwellings and Wilberforce Dwellings, they are shown here in photographs of c.1902.

277 (Right) 'Victoria Mansions' was the other major construction on Great Passage Street, designed by Gelder & Kitchen, and built by George Houlton. Based upon facilities established in London by Lord Rowton, it opened in August 1903, providing affordable basic food and lodgings for sailors and working men, as an alternative to the many squalid lodging houses in the area. It was used as a hospital in the First World War, and as army barracks in the Second World War.
The site was acquired by the Salvation Army in the 1940s, and re-named William Booth House following renovation in 1957. It was partially demolished in 1976 after a fire, and in 1984 the remaining buildings were also demolished. The present William Booth House was built nearby, still with the address of Great Passage Street.

278 (Below) This 1920s photograph shows the Nile Street playground, where children play on the converted bandstand of the Victoria Mansions' – visible in the background. The side wall of one block of the Artisans' Dwellings can also be seen on the right.

The foundation of Victoria Mansions was enabled by Charles Henry Wilson MP, who was made chairman of Victoria Mansions Limited, having raised £30,000 in capital.

279 A livestock market is recorded in Hull as early as 1599, when sales were restricted to the summer months, and held at various locations. In 1782 a more permanent site was created in Tan House Lane (later re-named Waterhouse Lane) with separate markets for sheep and cattle. By the early 1800s this site was used as a dump as markets declined, and it was not until the late 1830s that the more well-known cattle market was established in Edward's Place, on the site of former pleasure gardens. The Edward's Place market is seen here in the 1890s, looking north-east towards the Whittington Inn. The Whittington was established c.1800, no doubt to serve the pleasure gardens, and the original pub building was rebuilt in 1902, in the style we see it today. The Whittington is as popular as ever, offering food and accommodation as well as more traditional fare; part of the alignment of Wood's Lane remains on its southern elevation.

280 (Right) This 1920s photograph shows pens alongside the re-built Whittington Inn. The cattle market was extended and altered on various occasions but was running at a loss by the early 1960s. The last market was held in March 1989 and it then transferred to a site at Freightliner Road. The old site was re-developed as the Kingston Retail Park in 1990, demolition having begun in 1988 for the first buildings – including the Ice Arena and the Odeon Cinema.

281 (Below) At the south side of the cattle market was Edward's Place, laid-out on a former agricultural lane c.1836, as the market was built. This 1920s photograph shows the south side of the street, and housing in Edward's Square near the corner of Commercial Road. Running west from Commercial Road to Cogan Street, Edward's Place was mostly demolished in the 1950s.

next
K
next

The HULL BREWERY Co. LTD

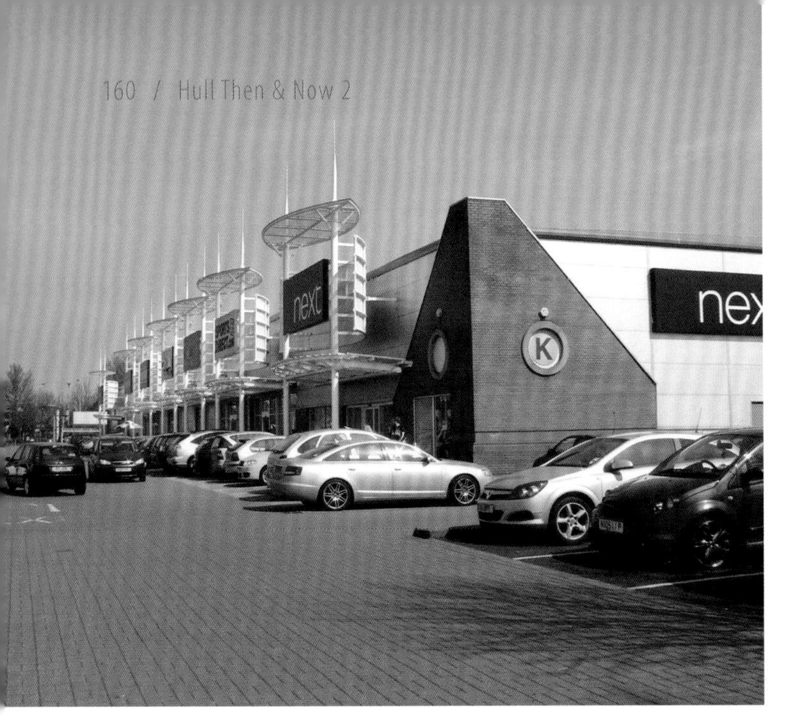

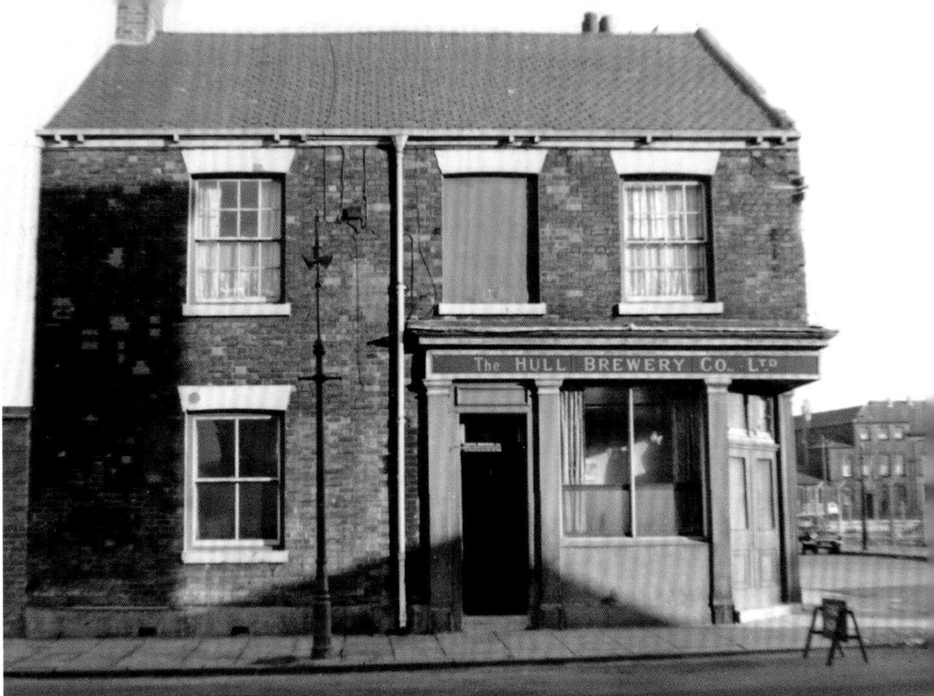

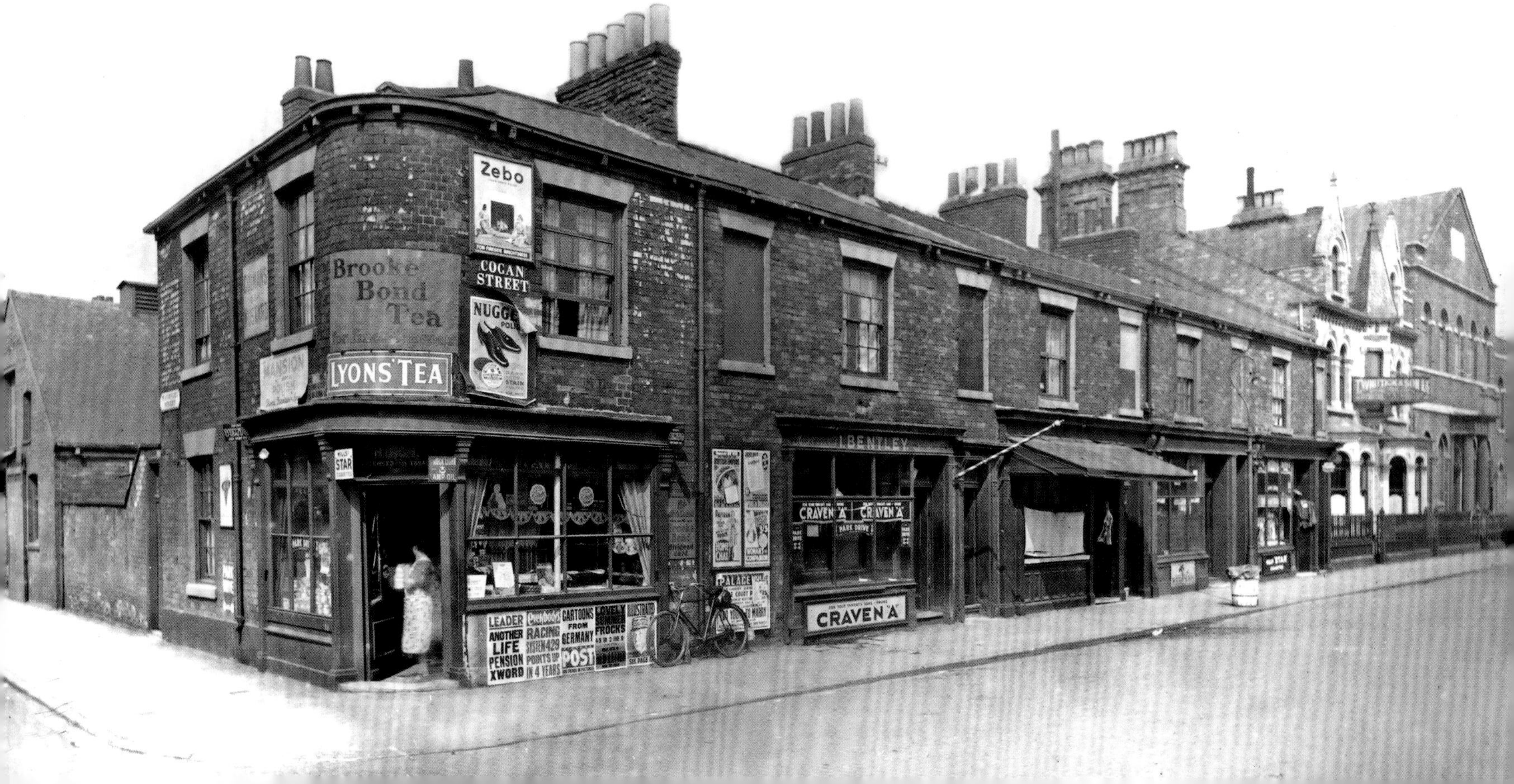
Zebo
Brooke Bond Tea
COCAN STREET
LYONS' TEA
MANSION
I BENTLEY
CRAVEN "A" CRAVEN "A"
PARK DRIVE
CRAVEN "A"
LEADER ANOTHER LIFE PENSION XWORD
RACING SYSTEM 429 POINTS UP IN 4 YEARS
CARTOONS FROM GERMANY
POST
PALACE

The alignment of Cogan Street was shown on Anderson's 1818 plan of Hull as 'Garden Cottage Row', as it ran to the west of market and pleasure gardens laid out there c.1800. At its southern end it ran into one of Hull's lost streets – Love Lane, which was 'paved and flagged' in 1809. The north end of Cogan Street still exists between 1950s flats and William Booth House, but its south end is now lost beneath buildings more typical of 2010.

282 The picture top right of the previous page shows a popular pub in this busy market area, the Commercial Tavern no.57 Cogan Street – the corner of Edward's Place. Built c.1840 it is shown here in 1956 when this area was being cleared of its blitz damaged buildings and 'slum dwellings'. Commercial Road can be seen in the far distance.

283 The main picture on the previous page shows property on the west side of Cogan Street, with the junction of Waverley Street on the left. This section of the street faced one of the entrances to the Cattle Market that led to the pig market area. The brightly painted and double fronted building along Cogan Street was the premises of T Whittick & Sons who were yeast merchants. Amongst the other shops that can be seen in the c.1930 view are Garton's shoe repairs, butcher Herbert Porter, and hairdresser Israel Bentley in the centre foreground. The shop on the corner was Alice May Hinch's newsagents at no.52. Just visible on the far right is the Salem Chapel that opened on Wednesday 3 July 1833, and was later used as a Jewish synagogue from 1914; it was demolished in July 1951.

284 (This page) Visible in picture 283, adjoining the left hand side of Whittick's yeast merchants, was no.44 Cogan Street. This small shop is shown here c.1900 when it was no doubt doing good trade as the Cogan Dining Rooms. It had been used as dining rooms since the late 1880s, and Charles W Harrison ran it from c.1895. It remained in use as such until the late 1920s, when it became a confectioner's.

285 (Above) Lister Street was laid out in 1829 and developed in conjunction with the church that was to be its focal point. The street probably took its name from Sir John Lister, who was a former mayor of Hull and a member of parliament, and is shown here in 1949.

286 The foundation stone of St James church was laid on Monday 14th December 1829, but by June 1831 discussions were still taking place as to the viability of erecting a spire on the tower – then still under construction. The church opened in August 1831, without a spire, remaining in use until the 1950s. Seen here c.1905, St James was demolished in 1957. St James Square is now a rare green space in an industrial area.

287 Porter Street was named after an ex mayor and sheriff of Hull in the late 18th Century, John Porter, who had land in the area upon which the street was partly laid-out. In September 1830 the Hull Packet reported: 'a number of new streets have been recently laid out in the Lordship of Myton, upon the fields at present occupied by Mr Lotherington. One to be called, we believe, Walker Street, is to run from the new church (St James) in a direct line north to the Anlaby Road. Another, to be called Porter Street, will commence at the corner of the Pinfold, and run in a north-east direction to the end of Osborne Street'.
Seen here in the 1930s is a section on the east side, showing the entrance to Porter Place, which bears a keystone dated 1844. Porter Street was gradually cleared from the 1930s onwards, although most of its alignment remains.
Flats built in 1938 (see right) sit alongside those begun in the 1950s, when a 'new 20 year plan' to improve the area provided 69 flats in three blocks. Hull's first 'tall' flats, built in Porter Street in 1955-56, seen as modern and desirable at the time, were later supplemented by further high-rise blocks built in the 1970s.

288 & 289 Great Thornton Street was developed from a rural lane that led from the Anlaby Road to an old pinfold, gardens, and at one time – the town gallows; hence it was variously called Gallows Lane, Pinfold Lane, and when developed from c.1840, Great Thornton Street. Its name was in honour of a Miss Thornton, who became the wife of John Porter who owned land in the area.

The foundation stone of a new Wesleyan Chapel was laid on the north–west side of the new street, on Wednesday 12 May 1841. The chapel took a year to build, and was designed in typical Greek Revival style by H F Lockwood, opening in 1842.

Seen below in 1904, the chapel was destroyed by fire in 1907, and a new chapel built on the site. Known as Thornton Hall, the new building is shown (right) just after opening in 1909, and was built to the designs of Gelder & Kitchen. This chapel was badly damaged during the Second World War, and subsequently demolished.

This section of Great Thornton Street is now lost beneath post-war housing developments and has been re-named Ice House Road.

290 & 291 The quality of the housing in Great Thornton Street varied wildly, but this 1920s photograph shows fairly typical property at nos.60 to 68, on the east side of the street. Reading from right to left – on the corner of Adelaide Street, was the Albert Dock Inn, which opened c.1872 and closed in 1953 as the area was being redeveloped. Then, at no.60, was the dining rooms of Mrs Margaret Tidswell, followed by the passage entrance to Gardner's Place. The former location of Henry Huckle's book shop was next door, followed by what had been the fried fish shop of Mrs Isabella Tomlinson; both converted back to private dwellings. A grocer Samuel Brodie was at no.66, followed by another private house, and on the far left two women stand in the shadowy passage that led to James Place.
The smaller photograph shows four of the six houses of Gardner's Place, viewed from the rear of nos.60-62 Great Thornton Street, shown below. Built in the 1840s, Gardner's Place was probably named after builder and bricklayer William Gardner of nearby Cogan Street, where he was listed in the 1840s trade directories.

As part of the plan to redevelop this area during the 1950s, the number of licensed houses (pubs) was reduced from 31 to just four.

292 Jane Street (named after Jane Porter) is now one of Hull's lost streets, but once ran west from the junction of Walker Street and Great Thornton Street, providing a link to the cul-de-sac Goodwin Street. This 1930s photograph shows the street looking west from the Walker Street junction to the Goodwin Street entrance. At the extreme right of the picture is a small part of the Queen's Head Hotel, which closed in 1958 and was demolished in 1967. The alley alongside the pub gave entry to Story's Buildings. In the centre of the next block was the passage entrance to Anne's Place, and then the wider open entrance to James' Terrace. In the distance on the right was the Walker Arms pub, which had its licence suspended in 1942 following Blitz damage. At the end of the street, where it curves south into Goodwin Street, can be seen the entrance to Petty's Buildings with the smoke cowls of a fish-curing house beyond.

The alignment of Jane Street is now completely gone, as this area suffered heavily during the Blitz and was cleared in the late 1940s leaving just the Queen's Head pub standing alone. The late 1960s redevelopment of the south side of the Anlaby Road required the removal of the last few remaining buildings.

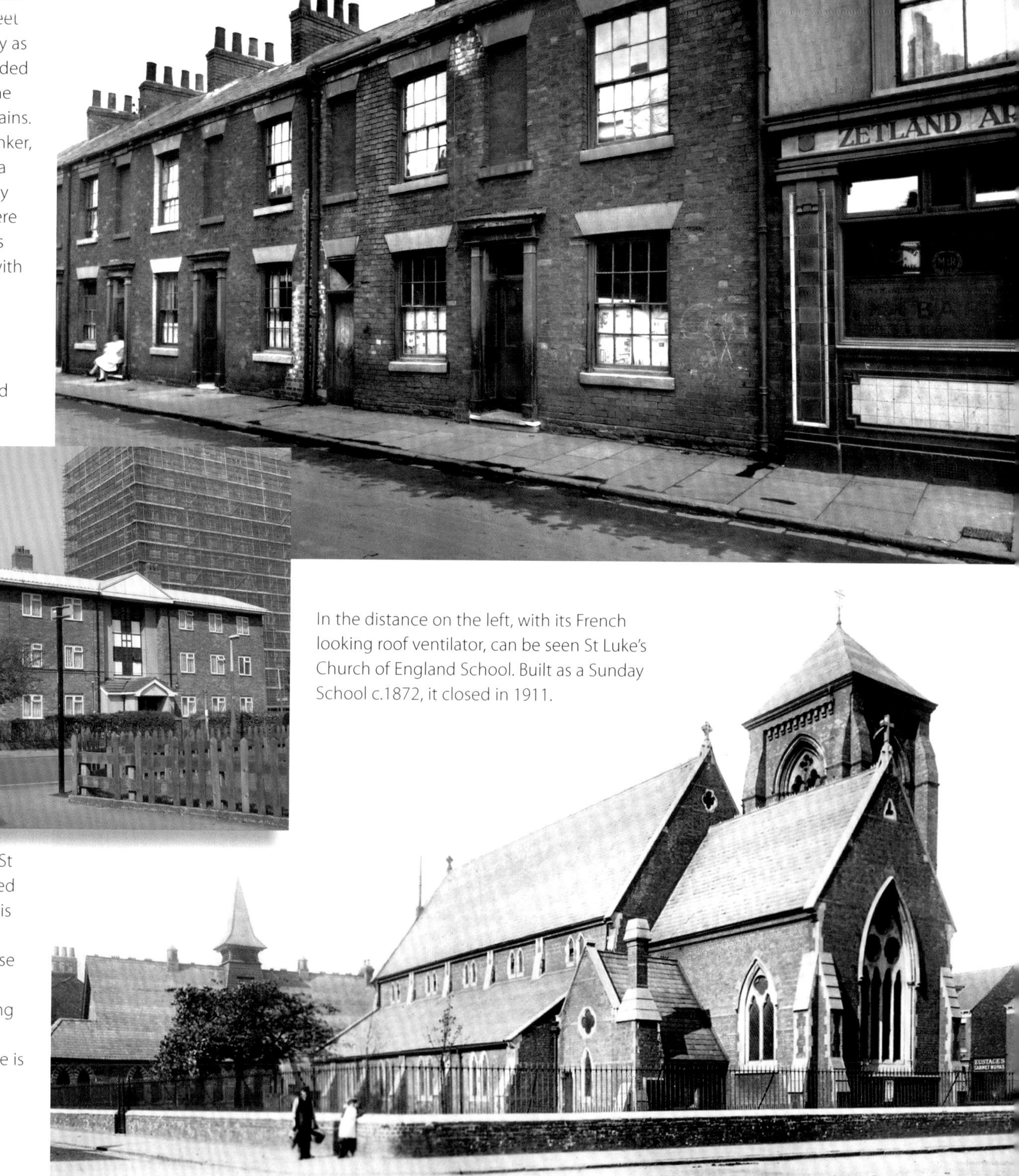

293 (Right) The existing section of Pease Street remains exactly as laid-out c.1860. Initially (from c.1844) the street ran from Adelaide Street (south) only as far as St Luke's Street, but was extended north to meet the Anlaby Road in the 1860s, and it is this section that remains. It was named after Hull's famous banker, Joseph Robinson Pease, possibly as a result of his investment in the Anlaby turnpike road. The section shown here in the 1930s prior to demolition, was on the east side, near the junction with Adelaide Street. Part of the ceramic frontage of the Zetland Arms, at the corner of Pease Street and Adelaide Street, can be seen far right, which closed in 1940 as the present Zetland Arms opened in Portobello Street.

294 Pease Street originally bisected St Luke's Street, but is now foreshortened to the small section that begins at this junction. St Luke's Street runs off the left of this 1904 photograph and Pease Street to the right. St Luke's Church, built in 1862 as Pease Street was being extended, was demolished following Blitz damage in the 1940s and the site is now occupied by 1950s council flats.

In the distance on the left, with its French looking roof ventilator, can be seen St Luke's Church of England School. Built as a Sunday School c.1872, it closed in 1911.

295 Michael Street, initially named Michael Place, was laid out c.1845 and ran off the south-east side of Porter Street. A cul-de-sac, consisting mostly of working class housing, the street's more presentable properties were at the entry to the street – shown here in the early 1930s. On the corner, at no.31 Porter Street, was the colourful shop of Charles Nicholson, who dealt in second hand furniture, specialising in pianos at a time when almost every home would have one. His sign proudly states that the Nicholsons had been in business over 50 years, however they were only at this shop from the early 1920s. Michael Street was demolished in the late 1930s, but is marked by New Michael Street, which sits roughly in place of the view shown here. However, the new street contains no houses and is simply an access road to the council flats constructed there in the 1970s.

A side-effect of the slower shutter speeds of the cameras used at this time, is the appearance of 'ghosts', such as the ice cream seller and children seen left and right.

296 Myton Street dates from c.1800 and runs north from the junction of Myton Place, Castle Street and Waterhouse Lane. It initially ran only as far as the corner of Roper Street, joining with the newly developed Anne Street c.1827, to form a link with Osborne Street. Myton Street is seen here c.1920, with Roper Street running off to the left.

Looking south along the eastern side of Myton Street, the shop on the corner belonged to baker Henry Schneider, and the names of other shop owners in the street at that time also reflected the mixture of nationalities that settled in the Myton area during the late 19th Century. Next door, sharing the same tiled frontage, was shopkeeper Israel Wolff, then – beyond the entrance to Agnes' Place, was hairdresser Isaac Marks. The larger building with pedimented door case was the newly built Myton Chambers.

What property remained in Myton Street after the late 1960s compulsory purchase blitz, has been systematically cleared in the last few decades in preparation for developments that have mostly failed to materialise. Despite the construction of one or two retail stores on the west side in the 1990s, a large section remains an undeveloped demolition site.

The 2010 view shows Roper Street bottom right, with Myton Street running right to left.

297 (Right) Lumley's Place was one of nine small courts on the north side of Roper Street; however, Lumley's Place was entered via a small alley off Myton Street, near to the Roper Street junction. This photograph, dated 29th November 1901, shows nos. 7, 8 and 9 Lumley's Place shortly before the housing here was demolished having been declared insanitary. The site is now a small car park at the rear of the Central Ambulance Station.

298 (Below) Roper Street was originally named Roper's Row, as it lay on the site of John & William Wells' rope works established here in the 1790s, hence its long, narrow alignment. The south side of the street, seen here c.1901, was unusual in that it had no court dwellings behind it, and ran as one continuous terrace of 34 houses from Myton Street to Waterhouse Lane. Seen here are nos. 47 to 59, again shortly before demolition in the early 1900s.

No.92 Osborne Street, with awning and tiled frontage was home to Samuel Kestenbaum, tailor, woollen cloth and trimmings dealer. This had formerly been a beer house called the Blacksmiths Arms, the last licensee being Thomas Taylor in 1910. By 1916 it was home to tailor Louis Rosenblum, and Samuel Kestenbaum by 1925.

299 & 300 Osborne Street took its name from Robert Osborne, a former Justice of the Peace and Recorder of Hull, Beverley & Hedon. Through his marriage to Sarah Jarratt he acquired land on which he laid out the new street in 1802, and rapidly divided off the land and sold it for building plots, that were quickly developed.

Seen above in the 1930s is a section on the north side, directly opposite the north end of Lower Union Street. On the far left was the entrance to Barker's Buildings, the interior of which is shown in the smaller photograph; the tall building at the back of the court is the rear of the former Hull & East Riding Club on the Anlaby Road, now incorporated within the recently refurbished Gilson Hotel.

The property seen here was demolished following Blitz damage, and Barker's Buildings is now the site of the Danish Church of St Nicholas, opened in May 1954. Any remaining properties were demolished for the southern extension of the Ferensway dual-carriageway in 1968.

301 Osborne Street begins at the junction with Waterhouse Lane, now shortened and blocked by the creation of the Prince's Quay Shopping Centre, which opened in March 1991. Behind the three Dairycoates trams waiting at the terminus, is the top of a pedimented building bearing a date stone of 1876. This was built as a Baptist Chapel in 1823, and re-fronted several times, latterly by the Methodist New Connexion in 1876. At the time of this May 1938 photograph the transit sheds of Prince's Dock were still visible over the hoardings in the background. On the far left of is an entrance to part of the former Hull Corporation Electricity sub-station, the large chimney of which was a familiar landmark from all around. Most of the buildings shown here were badly damaged during the Second World War and subsequently demolished, and the whole site is now occupied by Primark (formerly Allders).

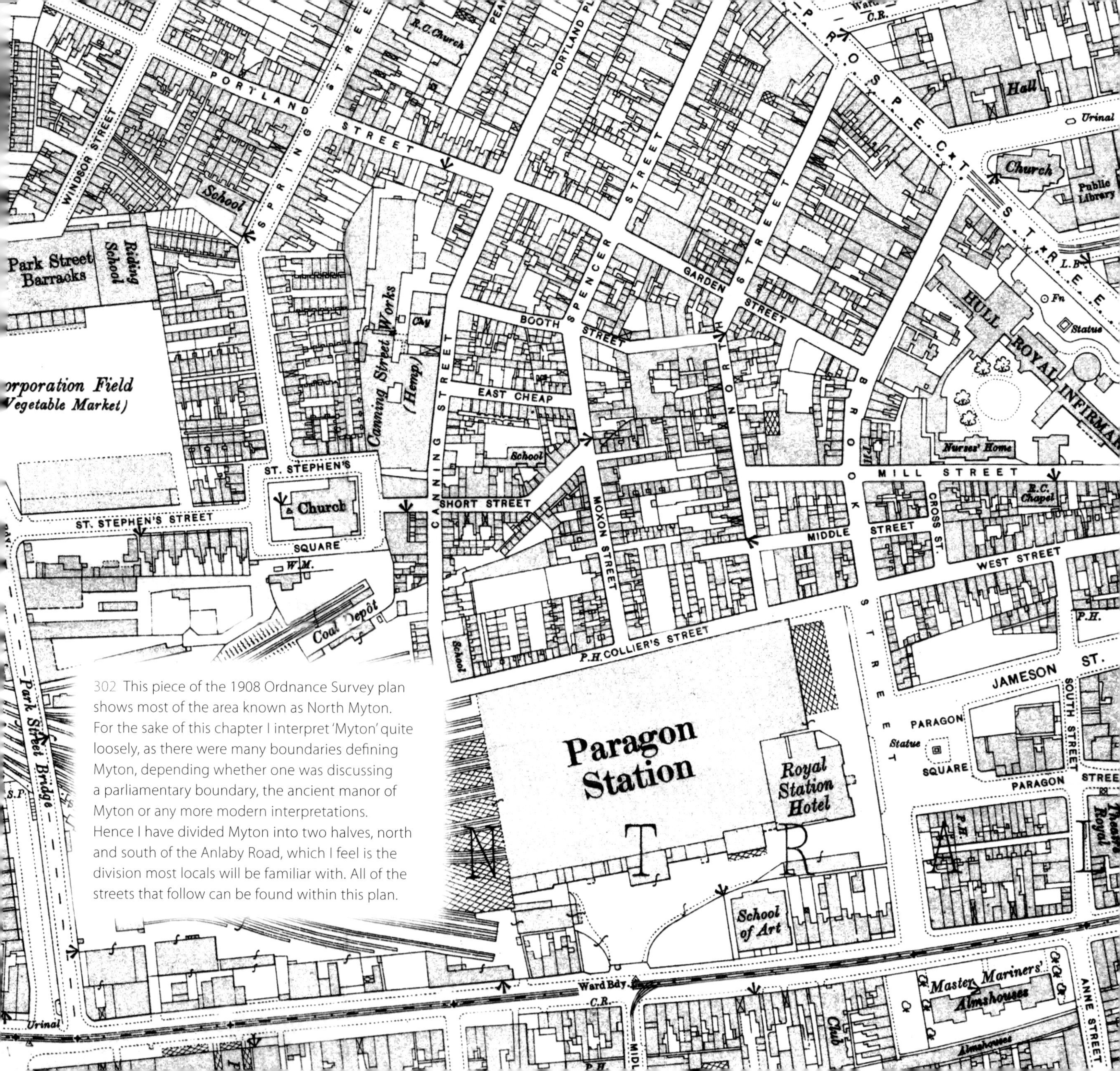

302 This piece of the 1908 Ordnance Survey plan shows most of the area known as North Myton. For the sake of this chapter I interpret 'Myton' quite loosely, as there were many boundaries defining Myton, depending whether one was discussing a parliamentary boundary, the ancient manor of Myton or any more modern interpretations. Hence I have divided Myton into two halves, north and south of the Anlaby Road, which I feel is the division most locals will be familiar with. All of the streets that follow can be found within this plan.

303 & 304 Dunford's Place was entered between nos.56 and 58 West Street, on the north side near to the junction with Cross Street. The court was originally known as Mary's Square, but was renamed in 1891, and is shown here in the early 1900s views facing north and south. The pictures show the six houses of the court, with (above) the two privies and ash pit used by the occupants. The walls of the court had been white-washed in an attempt to reflect what little light entered it, a tell-tale sign that it was a dark and depressing place to live. Only three properties were occupied on the evening of the 1881 Census, but 11 residents were squeezed into no.2, two residents into no.3, and eight residents into no.5.
The entrance from West Street is visible in the larger picture, and the site would now be beneath the southern entrance of the T J Hughes store.

305 & 306 West Street, now no more than a service road for city centre shops, was once part of a network of streets laid out in the open fields around Georgian Hull. Mostly built in the 1780s, a few of the houses on the north side of the street had front gardens, the evidence of which can still be seen in these 1920s photographs.

The photograph above shows no.26 West Street, the last property to retain its open garden area in front; no.28 to its left, has had a single-storey shop built on its former garden, which was a common practice during the 19th Century. Several examples of this can still be seen in Hull, for example the south-west side of the Beverley Road, where the first few houses set back from the road, still have their single-storey shops attached.

The second photograph (right) shows the continuation of the same terrace on the north-east side of West Street, leading towards the corner of Burden Street. What little remained of these properties, latterly just the derelict Star of the West pub and a Pet Shop, were demolished in 1997 as the Prospect Centre was extended. These locations are beneath the West Street entrance of the centre.

307 The next time you walk along South Street, heading south towards Carr Lane, pause a while and examine the entry leading to a tiny gated car park on the east side, at the rear of the Oxfam Shop on the corner. The area of the car park was once part of the site of Whipp's Court, which contained ten back-to-back houses, set parallel with the Carr Lane property; seen here in January 1908 are the fronts of nos.6 to 10. The 1881 Census records 14 inhabitants in the four houses here that were occupied that night. The tall building in the background is the Imperial Hotel, now the site of the Portland Hotel in Paragon Street.

308 & 309 (Above) The Full Moon pub at no.23 Spencer Street is shown here in a c.1910 photograph, possibly made when the photographer had partaken of a few drinks. It closed in 1922 and was demolished for the construction of Ferensway in 1931. As Ferensway opened, a new street called Lombard Street was created, alongside a new Corporation bus depot. The new buildings required the demolition of the section of Spencer Street shown top left, and some whole streets.

310 (Left) Eastcheap was one of the streets that were demolished for the construction the bus depot, and is seen here looking north with Spencer Street on the right, and the junction of Booth Street in the distance; also demolished. Eastcheap now lies roughly beneath the central arcade of the St Stephen's Shopping Centre.

311 Portland Street runs west from Ferensway as far as Colonial Street, its alignment relatively unchanged since it was laid out in 1827 across land once used as formal pleasure and kitchen gardens. It was named in conjunction with nearby Canning Street, as the Duke of Portland from whom it took its name, was a member of the government of Prime Minister George Canning, who died in 1827. This c.1910 photograph shows typical housing in the street. A short section of the street originally extended further west, beyond the line of Colonial Street to the back of the houses in Park Street; this was lost for construction of the 1960s office buildings, and most of the other housing in this area was demolished under late 1960s compulsory purchase orders. Just one original building survives in the street – the Star & Garter pub, established in 1872 by John Windass. Behind the unusual c.1930 frontage of the pub, is the original 19th Century building, a rare survivor in an area that is now completely given over to industry and retail outlets.

Thank you

The Sir James Reckitt Charity

Relay Port Agency Ltd • Import & Export Customs Clearances

Hull & East Riding Charitable Trust

Aflex Cables Ltd

Hull Civic Society

Hull Kingston Lions Club

Butler Tanner & Dennis • Printers

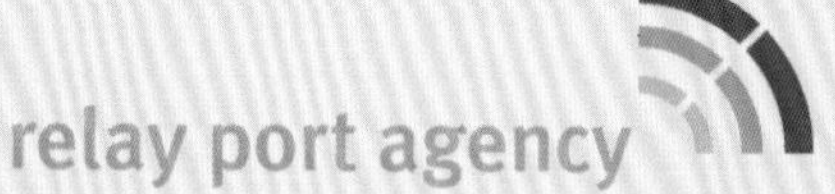

This book has been financed mostly from the funds of the Carnegie Heritage Centre. We have also been supported by sponsorship from the individuals, societies and companies listed above, and their generosity is acknowledged here. Some of our sponsors have again requested to remain anonymous and we respect their wishes whilst expressing our thanks no less sincerely to them.

Additional thanks go to the staff of the Hull History Centre, Martin Taylor for proof reading, Rob Barnard for proof reading and historic debate, Ian Halstead for technical advice regarding layout and design issues, and to Bobby Abbott of Butler Tanner & Dennis Printers of Frome. We must also thank Audrey Howes, the grand-daughter of Joseph Henry Hirst, for access to his note books.

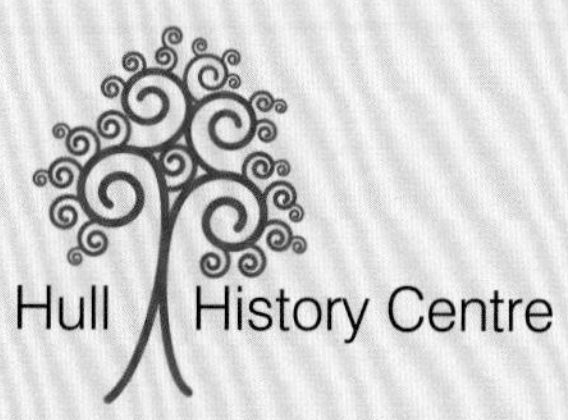

Of the 314 old photographs, maps and other illustrations used to compile this book, 220 are courtesy of the Paul Gibson collection, and where appropriate they have been supplemented by a further 94 from the following sources:

A Plan for Hull (see bibliography) 259

Peter Allsop 233

Frank Farnsworth 142, 207 - 208

Steve Goodaire 23, 37, 41, 48, 55

Audrey Howes Frontispiece, 3 - 11, 275 - 276

Hull History Services 1, 26, 38 - 39, 67, 143, 166, 176, 178 - 182, 190 - 191, 193 - 194, 196 - 197, 211, 226, 246, 248, 250 - 251, 260 - 261, 263, 267 - 268, 270 - 271, 273 - 274, 281, 283, 285, 287, 290 - 293, 297 - 300, 303 - 307

Hull Museums 177, 269

Bill Longbones 95

Mick Nicholson 49 - 50

Old & New Hull (see bibliography) 217

Ordnance Survey 185, 237, 254, 272, 302

Kevin Rymer 133, 137

Ted Tuxworth Estate 223

Rachel Waters 151

John Wiles 264

Bibliography

Victoria County History of the County of York and the East Riding. Volume I : The City of Kingston upon Hull. K J Allison (Ed.), Oxford University Press for the Institute of Historical Research. 1969.
Tremendous Activity in the Old Town; Demolitions Loss List 1943-1988. C J Ketchell, Hull College Local History Unit. Hull, 1989.
Forgotten Hull. G Wilkinson & G Watkins, Kingston Press. Hull, 1999.
Forgotten Hull 2. G Wilkinson, Kingston Press. Hull, 2000.
Boogie Nights, the dancing scene in Hull. P Gibson, privately published. Hull, 2001.
The Anlaby Road. P Gibson, The Friends of Lonsdale Community Centre. Hull, 2007.
Kingston upon Hull, The Second Selection. P Gibson, Tempus Publishing. Stroud, 2002 (re-printed 2005).
Victoria History of the Counties of England; a History of Yorkshire East Riding, Volume IV. C R Elrington (Ed.), The University of London Institute of Historical Research. 1979.
The University of Hull; the First Fifty Years. T W Bamford, Oxford University Press. Oxford, 1978.
Social Services in Hull; Being Institutions & Charitable Agencies of the City of Hull. Hull Community Council. Hull, 1930.
Adventures in Sympathy; Being the Story of the Port of Hull Society Since 1821. W Mawer, Brown & Sons. Hull, 1935.
Six Buses and a Tram to Nowhere. R Berriman, Hull College Local History Unit. Hull, 1998.
Sutton in Holderness; The Manor, the Berewic, and the Village Community. T Blashill, A Brown & Sons. Hull, 1896.
Evidences Relating to the Eastern Part of the City of Kingston upon Hull. T Blashill, A Brown & Sons. Hull, 1903.
Hull & East Riding Early Days on the Road; a Photographic Record. T Dodsworth, Hutton Press. Cherry Burton, 1987.
Lost Pubs of Hull. P Gibson & G Wilkinson, Kingston Press. Hull, 1999.
Architecture of the Victorian Era of Kingston upon Hull; Being a Study of the Principal Buildings erected in Hull, 1830-1914. I N Goldthorpe (edited by M Sumner), Highgate Publications (Beverley) Ltd. Beverley, 2005.
The Shop for the People, Two Centuries of Co-operative Enterprise in Hull and East Yorkshire. J E Smith, Hutton Press. Cherry Burton, 1988.
Landlord. G Wilkinson, unpublished. Hull, 2007.
Hull Pubs & Breweries. P Gibson, Tempus Publishing Ltd. Stroud, 2004 (re-printed 2007).
The Old White Hart Part Two (1673-1778). R Barnard, Hull College Local History Unit. Hull, 1999.
The Buildings of England. Yorkshire: York and the East Riding. N Pevsner and D Neave, Penguin Books. 1972 (second edition 1995).
A Plan for the City & County of Kingston upon Hull. E Lutyens and P Abercrombie, Brown & Sons. Hull, 1945.
Lost Churches and Chapels of Hull. D Neave, with G Bell, C J Ketchell and S Neave, Hull City Museums & Art Galleries and the Hutton Press. Cherry Burton, 1991.
Hull In The 1950s: A Pictorial Diary of Life in Kingston upon Hull. J E Smith, Hutton Press Ltd. Cherry Burton, 1994.
Horseplay in Westbourne Avenue; A History of Polo in Hull. M J Readhead, Hull College Local History Unit. Hull, 1998.
An Illustrated History of the Avenues & Pearson Park. C J Ketchell (Ed.), Avenues & Pearson Park Residents Association. Hull, 1989.
Grown in Sadness and Beauty; The Spring Bank Cemetery Walk. C J Ketchell, Hull College Local History Unit. Hull, 1998.
From Slough of Despond to Noble Boulevard; David Parkinson & The Westbourne Park Estate. C J Ketchell, Hull College Local History Unit. Hull, 1898.
The Want of Some Public Recreation Ground; Pearson Park. C J Ketchell, Hull College Local History Unit. Hull, 1995.
Newland Avenue Shops; A Survey. C J Ketchell, Hull College Local History Unit. Hull, 1995.
The Dirty Lane and the Fine Thoroughfare; Prince's Avenue. C J Ketchell, Hull College Local History Unit. Hull, 1995.
Newland Walk. C J Ketchell, Hull College Local History Unit. Hull, 1995.
Avenues Pubs. P Gibson, Unpublished. Hull, 1999.
St John's Wood, an Early Hull Housing Development. P Gibson. www.paul-gibson.com
The Pubs of the Stoneferry Area. P Gibson. www.paul-gibson.com
A Short History of Hull's Fountains. P Gibson. www.paul-gibson.com
Ideal–Standard; the First 100 Years. M Evamy, Staples Colour Printers. Kettering, 1996.
Streets of Hull; a History of Their Names (Revised Edition). J Markham, Highgate Publications (Beverley). Beverley, 1990.
A History of William Jackson & Son PLC. A Wilkinson, Hutton Press. Cherry Burton, 1994.
Illustrated Guide to Hull. E Wrigglesworth, A Brown & Son. Hull, 1890.
Inns of Holderness & Taverns of East Hull. J Wilson Smith (R Barnard Ed.). Hull College Local History Unit. Hull,
High Street Hull (1673-1798); Work in Progress. R Barnard, Hull College Local History Unit. Hull, 2002.
Old & New Hull; A Series of Drawings of the Town of Kingston upon Hull. T Tindall Wildridge, M C Peck & Son. Hull, 1884.
Kingston upon Hull City Council 19th and 20th Century Minutes. Hull History Centre.
Hull and East Yorkshire Trade Directories. Various. Author's Collection.
19th Century UK Census Returns. The Church of Jesus Christ of Latter Day Saints, CD-Rom. Intellectual Reserve. 1999.
History of the Streets of Hull. J Richardson, Malet Lambert re-print of an original series of articles in the East Yorkshire Times in 1915. Hull, 1980s.
The Hull Packet. Hull Libraries Online Resource.